Healthy Beginnings:
Your handbook for pregnancy and birth

Healthy Beginnings: Your handbook for pregnancy and birth is based on the SOGC Clinical Practice Guideline *Healthy Beginnings: Guidelines for Care During Pregnancy and Childbirth* and was adapted for the public and written under the direction of

Nan Schuurmans, MD, FRCSC, Edmonton, AB (SOGC President, 1996-97)
André Lalonde, MD, FRCSC, Executive Vice-President, SOGC, Ottawa, ON

Edited by: **Maryhelen Vicars & Associates**, Edmonton, AB

Designed by: **Halkier + Dutton Design Inc.,** Edmonton, AB
Illustrated by: **Arlana Anderson**

Consultants: **Members of the SOGC Clinical Practice - Obstetrics Committee:**
Guy-Paul Gagné, MD, FRCSC, LaSalle, PQ
Ahmed Ezzat, MD, FRCSC, Saskatoon, SK
Irene Colliton, MD, Edmonton, AB
Brenda Dushinski, RN, Calgary, AB

Acknowledgments: **Jean-Marie Moutquin,** MD, MSc, FRCSC, Laval, PQ
John Lamont, MD, FRCSC, Hamilton, ON
Geeta Sukhrani, MD, FRCPC, Edmonton, AB
Shirley Gross, MD, CM, CCFP, The Edmonton Breastfeeding Clinic, Edmonton, AB
Louise Aubrey, RD, Health Canada Nutrition Unit, Ottawa, ON
Janet McLeod for her invaluable help in preparation of the document
Royal Bank for support of this publication

Educational grant provided by **Janssen-Ortho Inc.**

Copyright © 1998 **Society of Obstetricians and Gynaecologists of Canada**
774 promenade Echo Drive, Ottawa, ON K1S 5N8
and **Cadence Communications Inc.**
759 Victoria Square, Suite 300, Montreal, PQ H2Y 2J7

ISBN 0-9698463-2-0

Important Information

Name:

Telephone:

Health Care Provider: Office Phone:

Office Nurse/Secretary: Answering Service:

Pediatrician: Phone:

Family Physician: Phone:

Hospital: Phone:

Address:

Ambulance   Telephone:

Breastfeeding Consultant: Phone:

Public Health Nurse: Phone:

Household Help: Phone:

Neighbour: Phone:

Partner's Phone during the day:

Expected Delivery Date:

Blood Type:

Appointments with my doctor or other health professional

Date	Day	Time
first visit		

This handbook is written and distributed by the Society of Obstetricians and Gynaecologists of Canada to empower women and give them the information they need to make good choices in pregnancy. It is based on the Society's publication, *Healthy Beginnings: Guidelines for Care during Pregnancy and Childbirth*, the guidelines Canadian doctors use in their practices to make decisions based on the most current research.

Being well informed about the ways your body prepares for birth and what your growing baby will need has been shown to make a big difference in how well your pregnancy progresses, and how healthy your newborn will be.

The advice and information in this handbook is "evidence based." This means that all the information in it is drawn from professional and credible research, rather than opinions or conjecture. The idea for this book came from international research showing that if pregnant women are aware of possible problems and how they can be prevented, mothers will have healthier pregnancies and more babies will be born full size, full term, and healthy.

How to use this book

Use your Healthy Beginnings handbook to read about what is happening and what is about to happen; write down any questions you still have and bring them to your next appointment. Use the journal spaces to take notes during your prenatal visits—especially if your partner is unable to accompany you.

Along with the standardized records your doctor's office keeps for you, the Healthy Beginnings handbook is an important part of your medical records. Record the changes in your body and your feelings for reference at the next office visit, or even months and years later, when your notes will remind you of this special time.

This book is not intended to replace the other good books, videos, audiotapes, or web sites that your doctor or childbirth educator may recommend. No book can take the place of medical advice and prenatal care that is tailored to your particular needs.

Table of Contents

SICK OF MORNING SICKNESS?

Get support from the Motherisk Nausea and Vomiting of Pregnancy (NVP) **Helpline.**

1-800-436-8477

Call our toll-free number for information and counselling
Visit the Motherisk website at www.motherisk.org for guidance

THE HOSPITAL FOR SICK CHILDREN

UNIVERSITY OF TORONTO

In 6 weeks a baby has a heart.
In 14 weeks, fingerprints.
In 22 weeks, eyebrows.
At this rate, it's a good idea to start
planning your baby's financial future now.

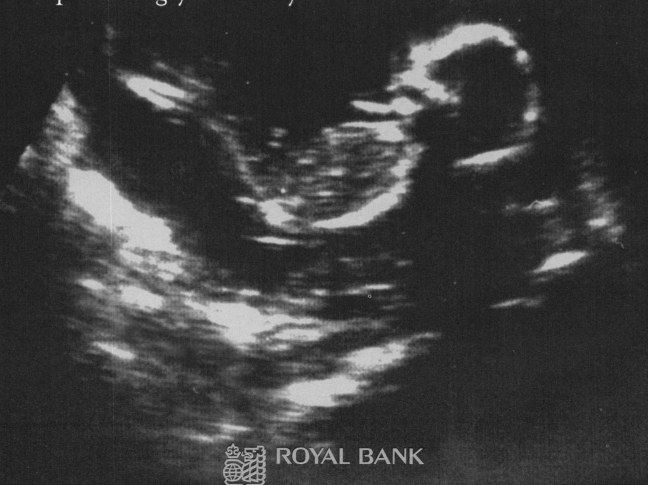

ROYAL BANK

Chapter One

Before you start your family

The menstrual cycle

The average menstrual cycle lasts 28 days. It may vary from 23–35 days. Almost every woman's cycle varies slightly from month to month.

Hormones produced by your body control the changes that occur throughout the cycle. They cause an egg to mature in the ovary and control the timing of the release of the mature egg (ovulation). Ovulation occurs about 14 days before your next period.

Hormones also cause the lining of the uterus (endometrium) to become thick with a layer of specialized cells and tissue. If your partner's sperm has fertilized the egg, this layer of cells and tissues acts as a protective home for a fertilized egg to grow and develop into a baby. If fertilization does not happen, the body sheds this protective layer during your next period.

If you are reading this book as you are planning your family and hoping to become pregnant, this chapter will help you give your baby a head start.

Most women understand how important it is to take good care of themselves and their unborn child once they are pregnant, but you may not realize that what you eat and how you keep fit now will also make a difference. In this chapter, we'll look at how your body prepares itself for reproduction, and what you can do to improve your chances of having a normal pregnancy and a healthy baby.

It all begins with an egg

At a certain point during a woman's monthly menstrual cycle, an egg will be released from an ovary. This is called ovulation. The egg will begin to move down the fallopian tube toward the uterus. If a sperm meets with the egg and enters inside, fertilization takes place and the woman is pregnant. The fertilized egg begins to grow at once by dividing into two parts, then into four parts, then into eight parts, and so on.

It will continue to move down the fallopian tube as it grows, and within seven days the egg will bury itself into the thickened lining of the uterus, which is called the endometrium. This process of burrowing into the lining is called implantation. For the first eight weeks, the fertilized egg is called an embryo. After eight weeks, and until birth, the embryo is called a fetus.

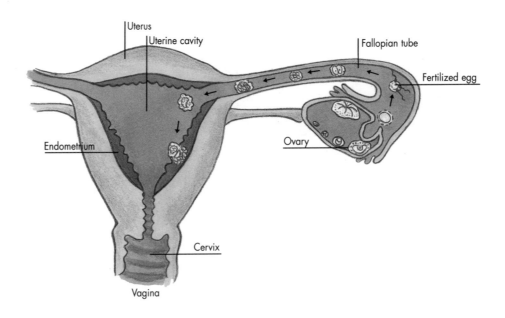

Uterus
Uterine cavity
Fallopian tube
Fertilized egg
Endometrium
Ovary
Cervix
Vagina

How your body supports new life

Within your uterus, the growing baby has everything it needs to live. It is protected in a sac filled with amniotic fluid. Its supply line to the outside world is the placenta, an organ made up of blood vessels and tissue that is firmly attached to the lining of the mother's uterus.

The placenta is the system that connects the mother to the fetus. The placenta begins to develop as soon as implantation has taken place and continues to grow throughout the pregnancy. When blood passes from the mother to baby through the placenta, it allows for the exchange of beneficial oxygen, nutrients and protective antibodies. On the return trip, the blood picks up fetal waste products that will then be transported to the mother's bloodstream for removal by her organs.

The placenta also makes and secretes a number of hormones, including estrogen and progesterone, that are responsible for many of the changes that occur in a woman's body during pregnancy. One of these important hormones, which only the placenta can produce, is called human chorionic gonadotrophin (HCG). A pregnancy test is considered positive if this hormone is found in a woman's urine or blood.

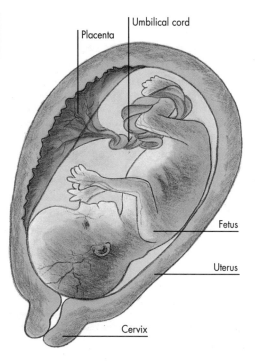

Placenta
Umbilical cord
Fetus
Uterus
Cervix

Did you know?

25% of women who have sexual intercourse without using birth control will get pregnant within one month

85% will become pregnant within one year

85% of babies arrive within a week before or a week after their due date

Early signs of pregnancy

Missed period

Feeling unusually tired

Tingling or tender breasts

Need to urinate often

Feeling bloated

Nausea (morning sickness)

Any unusual bleeding (different from your normal period)

Any one of these signs, especially when combined with a missed period, could mean you are pregnant (even if you have been using a reliable form of birth control).

Body changes during monthly menstrual cycle

(1) **A rise in hormone levels causes ovulation** to occur 14 days before next period

(2) **Lining of uterus begins to thicken** to prepare a safe home for a fertilized egg

(3) **Mucus secreted from the cervix** becomes more plentiful, clear, and slippery

(4) **The egg is released from the ovary** to begin its journey down the fallopian tube

(5) **Body temperature rises** for a few days just after ovulation

Keep track of your monthly cycle

If you don't already keep a record of your menstrual cycle, this is a good time to start. Mark each day of your period on a calendar, and you will soon have a written record that will help you to know what is normal for you and to discover when you are most fertile—and therefore most likely to conceive. Once you become pregnant, your knowledge of your body's cycles will help your doctor more accurately calculate the day your baby will be expected to be born (your due date). Your due date, and the date of your last menstrual period, is also used to measure how your baby is growing as the pregnancy progresses.

How easily you will become pregnant depends a great deal on your menstrual cycle. You are most fertile near the time of ovulation, and if you are hoping to become pregnant, you and your partner will want to have sexual intercourse around that time. But how can you tell when you are ovulating? The easiest way to tell when you will ovulate is to count back 14 days from the day when you predict your next period will start. Most women don't have to do anything different to get pregnant—for most, it happens naturally.

If you need to be more sure of the best days to try to get pregnant, you can watch for changes in your body that signal ovulation.

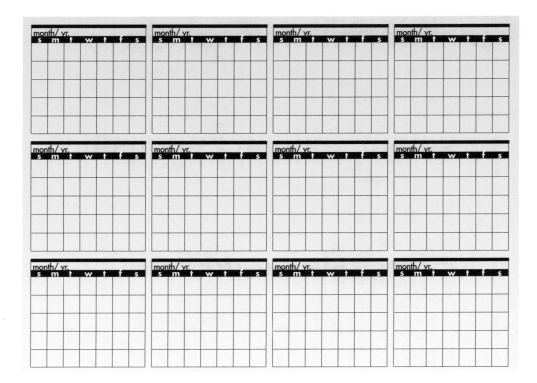

Evidence of a change in the mucus your body produces

On most days in the cycle, the cervix releases a small amount of mucus. But around the time of ovulation, this mucus becomes very clear, much more plentiful and very slippery—similar to the white of a raw egg.

Abdominal discomfort

Sometimes women experience mild lower abdominal discomfort or bloating during ovulation.

Visit your doctor *before* you get pregnant

Book a checkup with your doctor when you are planning a pregnancy. The most important reason is to try to prevent any problems with your pregnancy. You will be asked about your medical history, your family, the medications you take, your diet, your past pregnancies, your sexual history, and the kind of work you do.

If all goes well during this visit, you will probably not need to see the doctor again until you suspect you are pregnant.

It is important to learn as much as you can about pregnancy and childbirth. Studies have shown that the women who were most likely to have a satisfying childbirth experience were the women who had learned about pregnancy. These women felt the information they learned helped them to be more in control of their pregnancy and childbirth, and so they felt more fulfilled with the experience. In one study, it was clear that women who received prenatal education needed less pain-controlling medication during their labour, which suggests that they either had less pain, or were better able to cope with the pain they had. And yet another important study suggests that women were more likely to carry their babies to full term when they were made aware of the different risks that can cause premature births (page 40).

Regular prenatal care is important, but there is a lot *you* can do to give this baby the best of healthy beginnings.

I don't have to mention that, do I?

It makes good sense to be direct and completely honest about your health and lifestyle. Your health care team needs the whole picture to help you plan for a healthy pregnancy and birth.

Notes from your pre-pregnancy visit

_____

_____

_____

_____

_____

_____

_____

_____

_____

_____

_____

_____

_____

_____

_____

_____

_____

_____

_____

_____

_____

Recording your progress

Date: _____

Blood pressure: _____

Weight: _____

Exercise

You don't need the muscular strength and endurance of a triathlete to have a successful pregnancy, but being in generally good condition before you conceive will help you feel your best throughout your pregnancy.

If you have been active, ask about continuing your sports or workout activities safely. As your pregnancy progresses, your whole body is affected, and you may be more prone to injury. For example, you will need to limit high-impact activities and those that raise the body's core temperature.

If you have been inactive and want to get in shape now, begin gradually—perhaps with regular brisk walking, swimming, or other activities that will strengthen your heart and lungs and tone your muscles. Read more about exercise during pregnancy in Chapter 2.

Work

What type of work do you do? Women planning a pregnancy should take all recommended precautions when they must work with chemicals, solvents, fumes, and radiation. If you are already pregnant, your doctor may advise you to avoid any contact at all with some of these workplace hazards.

Very strenuous work, or working long hours and shift work, can sometimes lead to miscarriage, small, or premature babies. Read more about what is considered strenuous work during pregnancy in Chapter 3.

Nutrition

Eating well before you become pregnant will help your body meet the nutritional needs of your developing baby. Calcium and Vitamin D help to build strong bones and teeth. The recommended amount of calcium required daily for a pregnant woman is 1200 milligrams. Canada's Food Guide to Healthy Eating (1992) recommends 3–4 servings of milk products each day during pregnancy. One serving equals 1 cup of milk or yogurt or 1 ounce of natural cheese or 2 ounces of processed cheese.

Pregnant women and their growing babies will also need additional iron, protein, zinc, and B vitamins such as folic acid. These are found in red meat, chicken, fish, dry beans, eggs, and nuts. Protein helps to build strong muscles. Iron is needed to make hemoglobin, which is used by the blood to take oxygen to the baby. Women without enough iron have anemia. Before beginning any supplementation program, you should discuss your nutritional status with your doctor.

Canada's Food Guide to Healthy Eating (reprinted on page 8) is a good guide to follow both before and during your pregnancy. Its message to all of us is to eat a wide variety of wholesome foods every day. Establish good eating habits now, and you will find it easier to keep eating well throughout your pregnancy. Ask about vitamin supplements, including folic acid.

List the chemicals, solvents, fumes or other substances you must use at work.

Bring a product information brochure about the substance to your doctor if at all possible.

Name of substance and how you use it:

_____

_____

_____

_____

_____

_____

For more information about toxic substances that may harm your baby, talk to the team at the Motherisk Program at Hospital for Sick Children in Toronto by calling (416) 813-6780.

Nutrition quiz

If you check any of these, you have special nutritional needs that you need to talk to your doctor about.

- ○ I am following a diet to lose weight.
- ○ I "fast" on occasion.
- ○ I take part in very strenuous exercise.
- ○ I am overweight.
- ○ I am underweight.
- ○ I don't like milk or other dairy products.
- ○ I am a vegetarian.
- ○ I have a history of low blood iron (anemia).
- ○ I am a diabetic.
- ○ I have a serious medical illness which affects what I can eat.
- ○ I don't have enough money to buy the food I need.

Canada's Food Guide to Healthy Eating

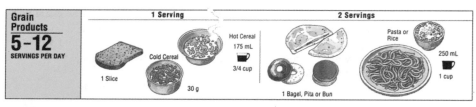

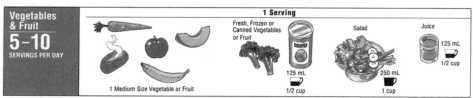

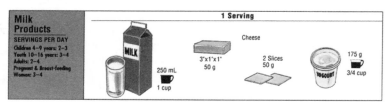

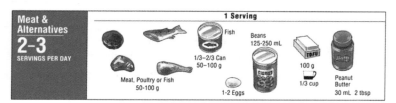

© Minister of Supply and Services Canada 1992   Cat. No. H39-252/1992E
ISBN 0-662-19648-1

Preventing birth defects with folic acid

Folic acid is a vitamin that has been proven to help prevent neural tube birth defects, including defects involving the abnormal development of a baby's spinal cord or brain—spina bifida, for example. These defects develop between the third and fourth weeks of pregnancy, in many cases before the woman even realizes she is pregnant. Taking 0.4 milligrams (mg) of folic acid daily before becoming pregnant, and for the first four weeks after conception, cuts the risk of neural tube defects in half. Women considered to be at a higher risk may be encouraged to take higher doses of folic acid.

Folic acid quiz

If you are planning a pregnancy and you check any box below, you should talk to your doctor about folic acid.

O I have epilepsy.

O I have anemia.

O I am an insulin-dependent diabetic.

O I have already had a pregnancy in which the baby had a neural tube defect.

O I take more than 0.4mg of folic acid daily, without a doctor's advice.

O I have a close relative who was born with a neural tube defect.

Good Sources of Folic Acid

Vegetables and Fruits

Amount	Food	Folic Acid
250 ml	Strawberries	.15 mg
250 ml	Raw spinach	.109 mg
250 ml	Cooked spinach	.262 mg
250 ml	Romaine lettuce	.076 mg
250 ml	Frozen peas	.094 mg
250 ml	Orange juice	.109 mg
250 ml	Cauliflower	.063 mg
250ml	Cantaloupe	.15 mg
250 ml	Brussels sprouts	.094 mg
1 spear	Broccoli	.123 mg
250 ml	Cooked beets	.09 mg
250 ml	Beans (yellow/green)	.15 mg
250 ml	Cooked asparagus	.176 mg

Meat and Meat Alternatives

85g	Cooked chicken liver	.655 mg
125ml	Sunflower seeds	.15 mg
250 ml	Baked beans	.15 mg
250 ml	Canned chick peas	.16 mg
250 ml	Canned pinto beans	.294 mg
250 ml	Cooked kidney beans	.229 mg
125 ml	Peanuts	.081 mg
250 ml	Lima beans	.156 mg
250 ml	Cooked lentils	.358 mg

Grain Products

125 ml	All-bran cereal	.043 mg
3 slices	Whole wheat bread	.075 mg

250 ml = 1 cup 125 ml = 1/2 cup 85g = 3 ounces

No thanks, my baby's too young to drink

Fetal alcohol syndrome (FAS) describes a group of abnormalities of babies whose mothers had a history of drinking alcohol during their pregnancy. These babies are smaller in weight and length. Despite good medical care, they do not catch up to normal babies. They may have small heads, heart defects, and poor control over their muscles. They sometimes show abnormalities of the face, limbs, and joints. They usually have some degree of mental retardation and/or behavioral problems, including hyperactivity, extreme nervousness, and a poor attention span.

Fetal alcohol syndrome babies are born with all, or most, of these abnormalities. If a baby is born showing signs of only a few of these defects and has them to a milder degree, the baby is said to have fetal alcohol effect (FAE). As fetal alcohol effect children grow up, they tend to have behavioral problems, learning problems in school, and trouble concentrating.

For more information about FAS/FAE, contact Canadian Centre on Substance Abuse at 1-800-559-4514.

Alcohol

Nobody knows just how much alcohol a woman can drink during pregnancy without causing harm to her baby. What we do know is that some babies will suffer serious birth defects if their mothers drink steadily or heavily during pregnancy. Alcohol-related birth defects can range from learning disabilities and personality disorders to poor growth and development, facial deformities, and central nervous system defects.

"Less is better, none is best."

This is not to say that a woman who has had a small amount of alcohol once in a while during her pregnancy should be worried. However, there are many different opinions about how much alcohol is a "small amount" and how often is "once in a while." How harmful a mother's drinking is depends on her own health, how much she drinks, and when. Most researchers suggest women avoid alcohol altogether during pregnancy.

Street drugs

It is important to understand that using street (illegal) drugs at any time during a pregnancy may cause damage to a developing baby. If used regularly, some of these drugs can even cause a baby to be born with an addiction. Babies born to mothers who use illegal drugs are usually smaller, tend to be more irritable and fussy, and may have brain damage that will affect their ability to learn.

If you are using illegal drugs, you need to stop before you get pregnant. If you have become pregnant while still using, tell your doctor. He needs to know about this, because you may need extra support and special care during pregnancy.

Medication

Almost all medicines, including prescription and non-prescription drugs, can cross through the placenta and into a growing baby. Very few medicines are known to cause any harm to a newly forming baby, although most have not been studied to rule out the possibility. The ones that do cause harm usually do so during the first few weeks of pregnancy because this is when the baby's main body systems form. Ideally, you should avoid the use of every kind of non-prescription drug while trying to conceive, and during pregnancy. Talk to your doctor first, before using any kind of drug, herb, plant, or home remedy. He will know, or can find out about current research into the safety of these products.

If you have a condition for which you must take prescribed medication, and you are planning a pregnancy, it is very important to talk about it with your doctor—preferably before you get pregnant. You may have to change the type of drug you take to one that does not cross through the placenta to the baby. If the prescription cannot be changed, the dosage may be reduced, or you may need to stop the drug during your pregnancy, if it is safe to do so.

Smoking

A link has been clearly proven between smoking in pregnancy and small or premature babies. There is a great deal of information to suggest that infants and children are also harmed by secondhand smoke. If either you or your partner is a smoker, an excellent way to prepare for being a parent is to stop smoking now.

If you are already pregnant, studies show that if you quit smoking before you reach your 16th week, there is less chance that your baby will be born too early or too small. Some researchers say your baby can still benefit greatly even if you quit smoking as late in your pregnancy as 32 weeks. As well, studies seem to indicate that by drastically cutting down how much you smoke during your pregnancy, you could increase your baby's birth weight.

You may feel that the risk to your baby is minimal. Some women may even feel a small baby is easier to give birth to. However, babies born too early and underweight are known to have a harder time adjusting to life outside the uterus. They are also more likely to have problems sleeping and eating, and they are more prone to getting sick. Ideally, if you are thinking about having a baby, you should try to quit smoking before you conceive. If you are a smoker, you may smoke as a relief from stress—a cigarette is a reward, a break, a way to feel calm. It may be hard for you to find better ways to give yourself a break, but there is support available. (See page 28 for ways to relieve stress.)

Be honest when you talk about your smoking habits. Ask about programs in your community that can help you to quit successfully. You may consider using a nicotine patch, if you have tried other methods of quitting without success.

Your medical history

Some illnesses or conditions a woman may have, or have had in the past, may affect the outcome of her pregnancy. Women who have serious medical conditions, such as heart problems, diabetes, high blood pressure, or epilepsy, may need to be followed closely throughout their pregnancy by a specialist in that field. Overweight women should be tested for diabetes.

If you, your partner, or another close relative has one of the diseases that run in families—such as muscular dystrophy, hemophilia, cystic fibrosis, Tay-Sachs disease, or beta-thalassemia—discuss this with your doctor. She may refer you to a geneticist (a specialist in the field of heredity).

German measles (rubella)

In the late 1960s, a vaccine was developed to protect people against German measles (rubella) and it has been routinely given to all preschool children ever since. The main reason for the development of a vaccine was to prevent infection during pregnancy, which can result in serious birth defects for a baby. Today, most women are immune to rubella by the time they reach their childbearing years, either because they have been vaccinated or because they have developed protective antibodies after being exposed to the disease.

Your blood will be tested for antibodies that show you are protected against rubella. If you do not have these antibodies, you may need to be vaccinated. It is best to be vaccinated at least three months before becoming pregnant.

Call these numbers if you need help quitting smoking or giving up alcohol:

_____

_____

_____

_____

_____

_____

_____

My medical history

Check those that apply to you:

O Problems with an anesthetic.

O Operations.

Please list all surgeries:

_____

_____

_____

O Blood transfusion in the year _____.

O Problems with my heart.

O High blood pressure.

O Diabetes.

O Problems with blood clots in my legs or in my lungs.

O A seizure-related disorder (epilepsy).

O Problems with my kidneys or bladder.

O Serious infection in the past.

Infectious diseases I have had:

_____

_____

_____

O A history of mental health problems.

O Problems getting pregnant.

O Allergies.

My family's medical history

List anyone in your family, including your parents, brothers, sisters, grandparents, and children, who has any of the following medical conditions and describe the condition.

Diabetes

_____

_____

A hereditary disease

_____

_____

High blood pressure

_____

_____

A deformity

_____

_____

Twins, triplets, or more

_____

_____

Other problems you think may be serious

_____

_____

Lifestyle and sexual history

You may feel uncomfortable with questions about your sexual habits, but, as with drug use, these questions are asked to help reduce risks to your baby.

If you have ever had sex without using a condom, particularly if you have had more than one sexual partner, you may have been exposed to a sexually transmitted disease, such as genital herpes, genital warts, chlamydia, gonorrhea, syphilis, or the HIV virus (which causes AIDS).

Some sexually transmitted diseases are curable; some are not. Some need to be treated to reduce the risk of infecting the baby at birth. Depending on your lifestyle and sexual history, certain tests can help you plan your prenatal care. HIV testing is now being offered to all women who are pregnant, and those thinking about getting pregnant, because there is effective treatment available for HIV-positive mothers to reduce the chances of giving their babies the virus.

Women who live with a disease that comes back again and again, such as genital herpes or genital warts, can still have a normal pregnancy. Sometimes, particularly around the time of the baby's birth, these mothers may need special care.

If you have been pregnant before

You will be asked about your past pregnancies and whether you had any problems during the months you were pregnant, during labour and delivery, or after birth. Knowledge of complications in past pregnancies can alert your doctor to try to prevent them from happening again. You can still have a normal, healthy pregnancy. It is again very important to give as complete an obstetrical history as you can, in case you are going to need special care.

Toll-free help line about HIV in pregnancy

Motherisk's toll-free HIV Healthline (1-888-246-5840) offers confidential counselling to Canadian women, their families, and health care professionals about the risk of HIV and HIV treatment in pregnancy. This new program also helps HIV specialists and community groups across Canada work together to help establish the safety or risk of HIV treatments.

I have been pregnant before

	1st	2nd	3rd
Date			
Name of hospital			
Hours in labour			
Delivery type			
Complications			
Boy/girl			
Birth weight			

What if I have been taking the pill?

If you are using any type of hormonal birth control, such as the birth control pill, implants, or injections, you should allow yourself at least one normal menstrual cycle before trying to become pregnant. This rest period allows your body to return to normal. To protect yourself from pregnancy during this rest period, use a condom. If you become pregnant while taking the pill, stop immediately, but don't worry. There are no known ill effects to the baby if this happens.

What about other forms of birth control?

You can stop using spermicidal foams, jellies, condoms, or a diaphragm at any time.

If you have an intrauterine device (IUD) in place, you should have it removed before you get pregnant. If you accidentally get pregnant with an IUD in place, you should have it taken out as soon as possible. Leaving an IUD in place during pregnancy is not a good idea because it can cause a miscarriage, an infection, or a premature birth. It is best to wait for at least one normal period to occur after the IUD is out before attempting to get pregnant. If you have an IUD in place and you suspect you may be pregnant, visit your doctor to find out if you really are. If possible, have the IUD removed. Sometimes the IUD cannot be removed for medical reasons. If that happens, you will be watched carefully for any problems it may cause.

Chapter Two

Well begun:
the first trimester

What is a trimester?

A trimester is a three-month time period, and is the term used for each of the three parts of a full-term pregnancy, which lasts approximately nine months. The countdown begins at conception, and the first trimester ends at about 13 weeks. The second trimester ends at 25 to 26 weeks and the third extends from about 26 to 40 weeks. The approximate date your baby will be born (your due date) is calculated by counting nine calendar months plus seven days from the first day of your last menstrual period. About 85 percent of babies arrive within a week before or a week after their due date.

The first trimester is a time of rapid fetal growth and development, and the time when your body adjusts to pregnancy. The choices you make about your health, diet, and lifestyle from now on will affect both you and your unborn baby.

Finding out you are pregnant can be one of the most exciting moments in your life, especially if you have been planning and hoping to become pregnant for some time. But the first weeks of your pregnancy may bring anxiety along with joy. What's happening to my body? What if the baby is not all right? Am I going to feel like *this* for nine months?

This anxiety is perfectly normal, but try not to worry. For one thing, you're off to a great start by using this handbook and learning as much as you can about pregnancy.

Your changing body

By the end of the third month, your body will have undergone dramatic changes. You may not look very pregnant yet, but you probably feel quite different. High levels of pregnancy hormones are responsible for almost all the changes your body will go through. From the moment of fertilization, your body begins to build a safe place for your baby to grow. This building process is complex, energy consuming, and the reason you feel so tired in your early months.

The curve of your waist is starting to disappear and your clothes feel snug. Your uterus slowly enlarges from the size of a kiwi to the size of a grapefruit. A mucous plug forms at the opening of your uterus to prevent infection-causing bacteria from entering the uterus during pregnancy.

Because of the milk glands now developing, your breasts feel fuller, heavier, and are tender. The brownish skin around your nipples will become darker, and will develop little bumps that produce an oily substance that keeps the nipples from drying out. The blood supply to your vagina and to the vulva (external lips of your vagina) increases rapidly and the skin of your vulva may turn a darker purplish colour.

Your heart works harder now because of the extra blood produced in your body that is needed for the growing placenta and to provide oxygen and nutrients to your baby. You may become more aware of your breathing or feel breathless as a result of hormone changes. Usually, your menstrual cycle will stop. If you have any bleeding during pregnancy, check with your doctor.

Your developing baby

By the end of this trimester, your baby will be 13 weeks old, about 9 cm long (3.5 inches) and weigh about 48 grams (1.7 ounces). At that stage, the baby will still have plenty of space to move freely and is very active, although you won't be able to feel movement until later. The baby will be fully formed and will need time for the body organs to mature and to gain weight.

At 13 weeks, the fingers and toes are developed. The bones are mostly soft cartilage but they are beginning to harden. The head still appears too large when compared to the rest of the body. There are signs of 32 tooth buds in the jaw. The heart beats about 140 times per minute. The lungs are developed and the baby "breathes" amniotic fluid. By 12 weeks the baby is already practising to suck by pursing the lips, turning the head and swallowing amniotic fluid, which is then passed as urine.

How often should I expect to visit my doctor?

An appointment every 4-6 weeks is appropriate for the beginning of pregnancy. After 30 weeks, visits should occur every 2-3 weeks. After 36 weeks, you should see the doctor every 1-2 weeks until you go into labour.

Your first prenatal visit

The first visit is usually more in-depth and longer than the rest. It may include a pregnancy test to confirm your pregnancy, an internal physical exam of your reproductive organs and pelvis, as well as a complete "check-up" of your whole body. Your doctor will listen to your heart and check your blood pressure. Your height and weight will be measured.

And you'll talk. Details about your medical and obstetrical history will be explored. If you saw your doctor when you were planning to get pregnant, you may go over some of the same topics you discussed then.

Why do I need to go to the doctor? I feel fine.

Prenatal care is the medical care you will receive before your baby is born. Although almost all pregnancies progress normally and most babies are born healthy, studies show that women who have regular pre-natal care have better pregnancy outcomes. Unless you have a concern that you would like to discuss sooner, set up your first prenatal visit before 12 weeks have passed since your last menstrual period.

Receiving proper prenatal care is an important part of making sure all goes well during your pregnancy. Regular prenatal checkups also let you become better acquainted with your doctor, and feel more comfortable in sharing concerns and asking questions.

With consistent prenatal care, he can identify problems early in your pregnancy and take steps to try to prevent any harm from coming to you or your baby.

The embryo develops rapidly during the first 8 weeks of pregnancy.

Notes from your first prenatal visit

_____

_____

_____

_____

_____

_____

_____

_____

_____

_____

_____

_____

_____

_____

_____

_____

_____

_____

_____

Recording your progress

Date: _____

Week of pregnancy: _____

Blood pressure: _____

Weight: _____

Fetal heart rate: _____

Talk it over

It is important to open the lines of communication with your health care team during pregnancy.

- Talk about your baby's father and the role he will play in the pregnancy.
- Tell them if you feel safe and loved.
- Explain how your family and friends feel about this pregnancy.
- Find out how you can take prenatal classes.
- Talk about breastfeeding.

Your doctor knows how important it is for you to be well informed about your pregnancy and your developing baby. But office visits, even this first long one, may not cover every topic. That's why you have been given this handbook, and why you will be encouraged to read other good books and to attend prenatal classes.

If you have just received this book, begin by reviewing the first chapter, which raises some topics that will be referred to throughout the book, including diet, exercise, and risks from alcohol, smoking, and other hazards.

What are all these tests for?

When you have your first prenatal visit, a number of laboratory tests are routinely recommended. These help predict risks to your health and that of your baby, and may include:

Hemoglobin: A hemoglobin test checks your blood to make sure it is able to carry enough iron and oxygen.

Blood group and antibody screen: This blood test checks to see what type of blood and Rh factor you have and looks for any unusual antibodies in your blood (see blood group and Rh factor on the next page).

Rubella titre: This blood test checks to see if you have immunity to rubella (German measles).

Hepatitis B surface antigens: A blood test to see if you have been exposed to Hepatitis B (read more about Hepatitis B on page 20).

VDRL: A blood test to screen for possible previous exposure to syphilis, a sexually transmitted disease.

Urine test: A test to check sugar and protein levels in your urine and to see if you have a urinary tract infection (chronic urinary tract infections have been linked to an increased risk of premature labour).

Pap test: Pap tests are done to check for cancer of the cervix or conditions that could lead to cancer.

HIV: A blood test to check for a possible previous exposure to HIV, the virus that causes AIDS.

Prescription and non-prescription drugs, herbs, and vitamins you take.

drug/herb/vitamin	amount taken	how often	how long

Remember to take this journal with you to every visit to your doctor.

19

Blood group and Rh factor

Your blood will be one of four types: A, B, AB, or O. A person's blood type is determined by the type of "antigen" attached to the blood cells. An antigen is a protein that causes a response from your immune system (the system that protects you from infection). Type A blood has only A antigens attached to its blood cells. Type B blood has only B antigens. Type AB has both antigens. Type O blood has none.

What is Rh disease?

Another antigen that sometimes attaches to blood cells is called the Rh factor antigen. If your blood has this antigen, it is Rh positive. If your blood does not, it is Rh negative. Only 15 percent of the population are Rh negative. But, if you are Rh negative and the baby's father is Rh positive, your child might inherit his Rh factor rather than yours, making her Rh positive too. If an Rh-positive baby is growing inside an Rh-negative mother, the two blood types are not compatible. Should the mother's blood and the baby's blood mix, such as at birth, or if bleeding occurs during pregnancy, the mother's body may react as if it had an allergy to the baby. It will begin to make antibodies to fight the Rh-positive antigens in the baby's blood.

Rh disease is rare

This blood incompatibility may lead to serious illness or even death for the baby. With advances in modern medicine, this incompatibility is now preventable, and therefore seldom seen. If your blood test shows there is a need to prevent your body from forming antibodies, you will be given Rh-immune globulin (RhIg) when you are about 28 to 32 weeks pregnant and again after your baby is born, or at any time during pregnancy if bleeding occurs.

Hepatitis B

Hepatitis is a viral infection that affects the liver. Hepatitis B, which can be sexually transmitted or passed to a baby during childbirth, is the most serious type to have during pregnancy. One of every 250 people has this disease. It is more common in people who have recently emigrated from Asia. Many people have no symptoms and therefore don't realize they have it. They are called chronic carriers and can pass Hepatitis B on to other people. A small percentage of chronic carriers go on to develop very serious and life-threatening liver disease.

Without treatment, about 50 percent of babies born to mothers who test positive for the Hepatitis B virus get infected—usually during the birth process or while breastfeeding. Without treatment, many of these babies will become chronic carriers as well, and a few may develop long-term health problems. To prevent this, babies born to mothers who test positive for Hepatitis B are now treated soon after birth with a Hepatitis B immune globulin, and with the Hepatitis B vaccine. In this way, 95 percent of these babies are prevented from being infected and from becoming carriers.

HIV

The human immune deficiency virus (HIV) causes infections and diseases that harm a person's immune and nervous systems. As people become sicker with HIV infections, they may be diagnosed with AIDS (acquired immune deficiency syndrome). Many people with HIV don't know they have it because they have never been tested for the presence of the virus in their blood. It can take five years or more for symptoms to show up.

The virus is found in an infected person's body fluids—semen, blood, vaginal secretions, and breast milk. Most commonly, the virus is spread from an infected person to a non-infected person during sex. However, the virus can also enter a person's bloodstream by way of a contaminated needle, so you are at risk if you share needles with an HIV-positive intravenous drug user. An infected mother can pass the virus on to her baby during pregnancy, delivery, or while breastfeeding. Very rarely, an HIV infection can occur from a blood transfusion. In Canada, this is no longer a high risk, now that the blood supply is carefully screened for the presence of disease.

You can reduce the likelihood of contracting HIV by limiting the number of sexual partners you have and asking questions about your partner's sexual history before you make love for the first time. Ideally, when you begin a new relationship, you should use a condom for at least six months. After two negative HIV tests by both parties, as long as neither of you has other lovers, you are probably safe to stop using condoms. If you use injection drugs, never share needles.

Do I have a lifestyle that puts me at risk for contracting a sexually transmitted disease?

○ I have had multiple sexual partners.

○ I have had sex with multiple partners, some of whom did not wear a condom.

○ I use illegal drugs.

○ I inject illegal drugs.

○ I have a drinking problem.

○ I participate in anal sex.

If you agree with any of these statements, you are at risk to contract a sexually transmitted disease and should be tested for the presence of an STD (including AIDS).

Take the test

The number of women of child-bearing age who are infected with HIV is increasing. Pregnant women can pass the virus to their unborn child or to their newborn via breast milk. Today there is treatment to help prevent this. Unless treated, many babies who are infected with HIV die within three years. That is why every woman who is pregnant, or thinking about becoming pregnant, should strongly consider being tested for HIV. Every pregnant woman in Canada should be offered HIV testing during pregnancy. If your doctor doesn't mention testing you for HIV before you get pregnant or during your pregnancy—ask to be tested.

Call Motherisk's toll-free HIV Healthline (1-888-246-5840) for confidential advice and support if you have been, or suspect you have been, exposed to HIV.

Chorionic villus sampling

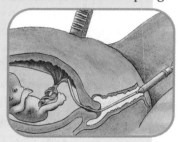

Amniocentesis

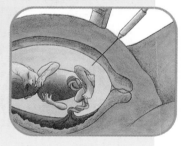

Ultrasound

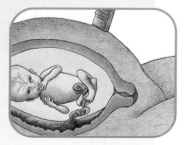

Genetic testing

At your first prenatal visit, your doctor may talk about genetic testing, unless you have already discussed the issues thoroughly at a pre-pregnancy visit.

Many factors determine whether you would benefit from genetic testing for fetal abnormalities early in your pregnancy. Your age, medical, obstetrical, and genetic histories are important. Any genetic diseases or birth defects your close relatives may have may also have an impact on your pregnancy.

If your family's medical history raises concerns, or if you are more than 35 years old, you should talk to your doctor about testing.

Testing may be done in one of two ways. One tests all pregnant women for certain conditions (maternal serum screening); the other offers testing to those identified as being at a high risk of giving birth to a child with birth defects.

Your doctor's advice will be based on your particular risks and attitudes, and on the availability of prenatal screening programs. Ultimately, the decision whether to go ahead with genetic testing will be yours.

None of the tests available today are 100 percent accurate. You may be offered some of these at your first prenatal visit, or later in the pregnancy:

Chorionic villus sampling (CVS)

This test is performed when you are between 9-11 weeks pregnant. A needle is inserted into the uterus, either through the opening of the uterus (cervix) or through the abdomen. A small sample of special cells (chorionic villi) is taken from the placenta for testing.

Amniocentesis

This test is done between your 15th and 16th week. A fine needle is inserted into the uterus via the abdomen. Ultrasound is used to help the doctor find a safe place to insert the needle. A sample of the amniotic fluid that surrounds the baby is taken for testing.

Ultrasound

This test is a screen for the entire baby. It creates a picture of your baby on a computer screen, using sound waves. Ultrasound is now routinely used to see the baby's position and how well it is growing, to discover where the placenta is attached to the uterus, to count the fetal heart rate, to see how many babies there are, and to check for some abnormalities. Ultrasound is also used to confirm your baby's due date.

Detecting genetic diseases and birth defects

If you, one of your relatives, or your child had a birth defect, try to find out the name of the disease and fill in this chart. Sometimes it can be helpful to mention this to your doctor before your 9th week of pregnancy.

Congenital heart defect _____

_____

Spina bifida _____

_____

Anencephaly _____

_____

Cleft palate _____

_____

Clubfoot _____

_____

Huntington's disease _____

_____

Born with extra fingers or toes _____

_____

Sickle cell disease _____

_____

Tay-Sachs disease _____

_____

Cystic fibrosis _____

_____

Thalassemia _____

_____

Hemophilia _____

_____

Muscular dystrophy _____

_____

Fragile x syndrome _____

_____

Other _____

_____

_____

_____

Call these numbers for dates, locations, and times of prenatal classes:

_____

_____

_____

_____

_____

_____

_____

_____

_____

_____

_____

_____

_____

_____

_____

_____

Who will deliver my baby?

Health care providers increasingly work in groups to provide 24-hour care all year around, despite holidays and vacations. In Canada, obstetricians, family physicians, and (in some provinces) midwives provide maternity care in a normal pregnancy. However, complicated cases are usually referred to an obstetrician. It is best to discuss your individual situation with your doctor.

All the information gathered during your pregnancy will be recorded on a special prenatal form. That way, any nurse, doctor, midwife, or other health care provider who reviews your prenatal record can be brought right up to date about your pregnancy.

Prenatal classes

Many thousands of women and their families take part in prenatal classes every year. Maybe this is because women report feeling more confident when they understand the changes pregnancy brings. Or perhaps it is simply because prenatal classes bring women and their families together and give them a chance to share their experiences, wisdom, and feelings. Certainly learning about pregnancy helps women to make informed decisions about their pregnancy and childbirth.

At one time, prenatal classes focused on the stages of labour and pain control during delivery. Today's classes still deal with these topics, but they also cover prenatal nutrition, parenting skills, signs of problems, exercise during pregnancy, and sexual relations during pregnancy. Classes are particularly helpful to women who are having their first baby and to young women who are pregnant during their teen years. Expectant fathers can learn about their changing relationship with their partners and their new role as a parent. Children can learn to be prepared for the arrival of a new brother or sister.

If you are more comfortable learning in a language other than English, you may be able to find prenatal classes that are offered in different languages and will take into consideration the participants' ethnic and cultural backgrounds. There are often classes for teens.

Some communities offer postnatal classes to help families adjust to their new baby by exploring issues such as breastfeeding, getting back into shape, sexuality after pregnancy, and normal infant growth and development.

If you are interested in taking part in prenatal or postnatal classes, ask your doctor where to sign up in your area.

Common discomforts in early pregnancy

Nausea and vomiting

The cause of "morning sickness" is still not known. Usually it occurs during the first three or four months of pregnancy, but it can linger. You may feel nauseated at any time during the day or night—particularly when your stomach is empty.

For most women, the feeling of nausea and episodes of vomiting reduce enough at some point during the day to allow them to feel hungry again and to keep food down. However, one percent of pregnant women in Canada—about 4000 women per year—will suffer from such severe nausea and vomiting that the lack of foods, fluids, and nutrients may be harmful to their health and the well-being of their baby.

If left untreated, severe nausea and vomiting can lead to weight loss and aggravation of electrolyte imbalance. Electrolytes are substances that play an important role in making sure that the body works normally. Imbalances in the level of electrolytes such as sodium, calcium, chloride, magnesium, and phosphate can lead to health problems for pregnant women and their babies.

For these reasons, it is important to talk to a doctor if you have severe nausea and vomiting during pregnancy.

Medication for nausea and vomiting

Although you are quite right to stay away from over-the-counter medications when you're pregnant, a new prescription medication can help. Doxylamine Succinate Pyridoxine HCl (Diclectin®) was specially prepared to treat this condition in pregnant women. It is made up of two parts: Vitamin B6 and an antihistamine called doxylamine. It is the most studied medication of its kind in the world. The Society of Obstetricians and Gynaecologists of Canada and the Motherisk Program at the Hospital for Sick Children in Toronto recognize this medication as a safe and effective treatment for nausea and vomiting during pregnancy.

Getting help for morning sickness

The Motherisk Program, based at the Hospital for Sick Children in Toronto, is made up of a group of world-renowned experts who study the effects medications and diseases have on pregnancy. They are now conducting a study on the effects of nausea and vomiting during pregnancy (NVP) on the health of expectant mothers and their unborn children. If you are currently experiencing nausea and vomiting during your pregnancy, the Motherisk Program team will be pleased to share information with you on ways to deal with morning sickness.

Call the Motherisk NVP Helpline toll free at 1-800-436-8477.

If you have access to the World Wide Web, go to the Motherisk Program's web site. www.motherisk.org

How to get out of making dinner— and other un-sickening ideas

Here are a few tips that may be helpful to settle your stomach:

Avoid smells that make you feel nauseated—such as cooking odours or perfume. Get your partner to prepare meals if possible.

Eat whatever food you want that looks and smells appealing and that relieves your nausea.

Avoid warm places because feeling hot can add to nausea.

Sniffing fresh lemons or ginger, drinking lemonade, or eating watermelon slices seems to help.

Eating salty potato chips has been found to help settle stomachs enough to eat a meal.

Acupressure treatment has been beneficial to many women to help control nausea and vomiting.

Tender, painful breasts

The most important thing you can do is get a good support bra and wear it all the time, even at night. Make sure it fits properly and that it has full, rounded cups with wide, non-elastic shoulder straps. Warm compresses sometimes help, and if your nipples are sore, try applying some moisturizing cream.

Tiredness

Two things cause the unusual tiredness many women feel during the first few months. First, your metabolism has increased, which is very energy consuming. Second, one of the pregnancy hormones (progesterone) has a sedative effect. The best advice is not to fight it. Pay attention to your body when you feel you need rest, or even a nap. Many women who "never nap" find themselves suddenly very ready for a little daytime rest. If it is possible at your workplace, try to find a quiet place to put your feet up and close your eyes when you have breaks. If this is impossible, plan to lie down as soon as you get home from work.

How to get out of changing Tigger's litter box

Toxoplasmosis is a disease caused by a microscopic parasite that lives in a host animal and is passed on to other animals through feces. Up to half the world's human population has been exposed to the parasite, but it is rare for an adult to have any symptoms. There is a small risk of birth defects in a baby born to a mother exposed to the parasite during her pregnancy.

Just to be on the safe side, avoid eating undercooked meat or chicken when you are pregnant, and wear rubber gloves when you handle raw meat or chicken. If you have a cat, try to have someone else change the litter box. If you must do it, wear gloves, avoid inhaling the dust, and wash your hands well afterwards.

Headaches

Headaches are quite common during pregnancy and they are not usually cause for alarm. However, if you have headaches that are constant, very severe, cause blurred vision, nausea, or spots to appear in front of your eyes, you should contact your doctor.

If you have a headache, try lying down in a dark, cool room. Place a cool cloth on your forehead. Ask your partner for a neck and back massage. You can also try eating small meals often—sometimes the headache is related to low blood sugar, especially if you are feeling nauseated and don't feel like eating. If you take plain acetaminophen (for example, Tylenol®) tablets occasionally, you will not harm your baby.

Frequent urination

Have you found yourself heading for the bathroom a lot more often lately? It is a normal feature of early pregnancy to frequently have the urge to urinate. This is caused by the growing uterus putting pressure on your bladder and the increased amount of urine being produced by your kidneys. You may feel as though your bladder is very full but then, when you go to the washroom, you find you only pass a little urine. Sometimes this pressure causes urine to leak out when you move or cough. Kegel exercises may help (see page 34). If you feel any pain when you urinate, you need to have this checked out—you may have an infection.

Bleeding

Some women have some harmless spotting in the early months of pregnancy, and go on to deliver healthy babies, but if you have any bleeding at all you should take it seriously, as it may be a sign of possible miscarriage. Get in touch with your doctor.

Losing a baby through miscarriage happens in about 15 percent of pregnancies. A miscarriage seems to be the body's way of ending a pregnancy that is not developing normally. A miscarriage will not usually prevent a woman from having a normal pregnancy in the future but it is best to wait at least one menstrual cycle before trying again.

Fainting

Feeling faint is common during pregnancy and is probably explained by the combination of increased hormone levels, your changing circulatory system, and low blood sugar levels. If you feel lightheaded, try eating something sweet. Eating small nutritious meals and snacks can help alleviate this. When you feel faint, sit down and put your head between your knees. Loosen any tight clothing and place a cool, wet cloth on your forehead or the back of the neck. If the feeling persists, call your doctor.

About weight gain

Researchers have not determined the exact amount of weight a woman should gain during pregnancy.

Most women gain somewhere between 6.8 kg (15 pounds) and 18.2 kg (40 pounds). However, a woman can gain more or less than those amounts and still have a perfectly normal pregnancy and childbirth.

Eating a healthy well-balanced diet is much more important than counting calories and worrying about whether you are gaining too much or too little weight. How much weight you gain has nothing to do with how big or small your baby will be. What we do know is that women should not diet during pregnancy, even if they are overweight before the pregnancy. Women who are underweight and teenagers, in particular, should eat heartily, properly, and often.

For more information about nutrition and pregnancy, see page 7. If you have an internet connection, try the links from **www.motherisk.org** .

Call these numbers for a dietitian who can answer your nutrition questions:

_____

_____

_____

_____

_____

_____

_____

Special calorie considerations

During pregnancy all women should eat a balanced, healthy diet and take in between 2200 and 2400 calories per day. However, if you exercise regularly, this may not be enough and you should eat more than 2400 calories a day. In addition, it is recommended that you increase your complex carbohydrates (such as rice, pasta and potatoes) to make up 30–40 percent of your total caloric intake.

About abuse

One in 12 women in Canada is a victim of physical violence. A staggering 40 percent of wife assault incidents begin during the time of a woman's first pregnancy. Physical abuse during pregnancy can cause serious injuries to the mother and cause her baby to be born too early and too small. Some unborn babies have died because of a beating their mothers survived.

If you are pregnant and a victim of physical abuse, you probably feel very alone. You need help now.

No one deserves to be abused. Sometimes, abuse in a family can leave a woman feeling embarrassed and ashamed, and even that the abuse was her fault. If this is your situation, please ask for help. Talk to your doctor, who will appreciate your courage and help you find the community resources you will need.

About stress and your support group

Everyone has some stress in their life but having too much stress is not healthy, particularly during pregnancy. Research has shown that stress in pregnant women may be associated with premature birth and too-small babies.

How much support you receive from the people around you can have a direct effect on how much stress you feel during your pregnancy. If you receive very little support, you may feel lonely and depressed.

Although pregnancy is a joyous time for most couples, the change and adjustments can sometimes cause strain within your relationship. Unexpected life events may increase your stress levels. If this happens to you, get help.

Ways to reduce your stress

Women with too much stress need to learn healthy ways to deal with it.

1. **Share the joys, challenges, and worries of pregnancy** with someone close to you—this can make your pregnancy seem less stressful. If, for whatever reason, you don't have the support of your partner, try to spend time with other people you enjoy.

2. **Attend prenatal classes and meet other women** going through pregnancy. The breathing and concentration exercises taught for childbirth can help you relax now.

3. **Get active. Exercise** has been proven to lift the spirits and reduce stress.

4. **Get enough sleep.**

5. **Learn other rest and relaxation techniques** by reading books and listening to audiotapes, available in most public libraries.

6. **Knowledge and preparation can reduce the anxiety you may be feeling** about the birth itself. Working with your health care provider and support person to prepare a birth plan may help. Read about birthing plans on pages 60-64.

Diabetes and pregnancy

Your body produces, in the pancreas, the substance insulin. Insulin is needed to make sure that sugar (glucose) is able to get inside your body's cells to produce energy. Without insulin, the glucose would remain in your blood. If too much glucose is in your bloodstream, you will have high blood glucose levels and no energy production in your cells.

Energy is needed to make all of your body organs work properly, including your lungs, brain, and your heart and blood vessels.

A mild diabetic has a pancreas that produces some insulin, but not enough to move all the glucose they need into their cells. These people are able to control their blood glucose levels by eating properly and by getting regular exercise to burn off the extra glucose. Some diabetics cannot produce any insulin in their pancreas at all, and must take insulin by injection in order for any glucose to reach the inside of their cells. Without insulin, a person cannot live.

If you have insulin-dependent diabetes

When a person's pancreas does not produce any insulin, he or she must get insulin from somewhere else in order to survive—most commonly synthetic insulin. This person is said to have Insulin Dependent Diabetes Mellitus (IDDM), also called Type I diabetes. They must test their blood glucose levels every day, and then inject the right amount of insulin to keep their blood glucose levels normal. For some people, having good control of their blood glucose levels is not always easy. When an insulin-dependent woman becomes pregnant, this challenge becomes even greater. Good control of blood glucose levels is very important for a healthy pregnancy, especially in the month of conception and in the first trimester. Babies born to mothers whose blood glucose levels are not under tight control during their entire pregnancy may be unusually large (4.5 kg/10 lbs. or more) and hard to deliver, or they may have birth defects. For these reasons, insulin-dependent diabetics should see a specialist (obstetrician) during a pregnancy.

Notes from your prenatal visit at 10 to 16 weeks

This visit is scheduled for about four weeks after the first one. You will usually not have an extensive physical examination, but you will be weighed and have your blood pressure taken. The doctor will check for the growth of the uterus and may check the baby's heart rate.

You and your doctor will discuss the results of any tests that were ordered at the previous visit. If there is any further testing or other action needed, you'll talk about that.

Your responsibility, as at every prenatal visit, is to be aware of your own concerns and ask questions. This handbook will help. You will have your notes from the last visit, and any questions that have occurred to you in the meantime.

If possible, it is good for the expectant father to go with the mother to the doctor's visit at least once. He will meet the person who is caring for his partner and ask about some of the concerns he has about the pregnancy. Other partners welcome to attend prenatal visits with you are a close friend, your mother, or another family member.

Recording your progress

Date: _____

Week of pregnancy: _____

Blood pressure: _____

Weight: _____

Fetal heart rate: _____

About sex

With pregnancy, many women experience a change in their levels of sexual desire, especially during this first trimester. Your hormones are making breasts and vulva more sensitive, and this may make lovemaking more attractive than ever; fatigue, nausea, and vomiting may make it the furthest thing from your mind. Don't worry—if you are in either camp, you have lots of company.

Some couples feel closer than ever during this special time and continue to have enjoyable lovemaking until just before their baby is due. Other couples feel their relationship is strained as a result of all the changes taking place and find that sex is not as fulfilling during pregnancy. Your partner may be worried that having sex could harm the baby.

If either of you is reluctant to make love, make time for other kinds of physical intimacy that may still appeal: cuddling, holding hands, massage, or bathing together, for example.

Usually, having intercourse will not harm the pregnancy in any way. However, your doctor may advise you to avoid or limit intercourse if you have an infection, problems with bleeding, or problems with leaking amniotic fluid or the breaking of the amniotic sac. But that doesn't have to mean no lovemaking. If you feel like it, explore alternatives to vaginal sex, such as mutual masturbation or oral sex. Just a warning about oral sex—ask your partner to be careful not to blow any air into your vagina. Doing this could force air into your bloodstream and cause an air embolism, that could be fatal to both you and your baby.

About exercise during pregnancy

There are different kinds of "workouts" that can be part of your daily routine, now that you are pregnant: aerobic exercise (with caution), strength training, relaxation techniques, and Kegel exercises.

Aerobic exercise

Exercise that is strenuous enough to make your heart beat more quickly than when you are resting is called aerobic. It can include brisk walking, jogging, cycling, swimming, or team sports.

When is it not safe to exercise?

You should not exercise during this pregnancy if any of these conditions apply to you, until you have discussed your answers with your doctor.

Heart problems.

A serious lung condition and breathing problems.

High blood pressure.

Some vaginal bleeding during this pregnancy.

Low blood iron (anemia).

Carrying more than one baby.

Problems controlling (or my doctor is concerned about) my blood sugar.

My doctor has told me my baby is too small for its age in my uterus.

A lot of lower back pain.

Discomfort in the bones of my pelvis.

If you have been active before, you can probably continue with the same or a modified level of activity. But clear your exercise plans with your doctor as early in your pregnancy as possible, so she can rule out any conditions that would make vigorous exercise risky.

In general, avoid working out at a level that leaves you exhausted, thirsty, or too hot. Animal studies show that a sudden rise in your core body temperature during the early weeks of pregnancy may harm the baby.

So how can you tell if you are overexerting yourself? Try the "talk test." You should always be able to carry on a conversation during your workout. If not, you are working too hard.

If you get the green light from the doctor, go for it. Walk, swim, or join a fitness class, especially one that is designed for pregnant women and new mothers. If you are in a regular aerobics class, speak to your instructor about avoiding routines that are high-impact, or that put stress on your lower back.

Suggested heart rate target zones for aerobic exercise in pregnancy

Mother's Age	Heart Rate Target
Less than 20 years	140 – 155
20 - 29 years	135 – 150
30 - 39 years	130 – 145
More than 40 years	125 – 140

This applies to most healthy pregnant women. At the beginning of a new exercise or late in your pregnancy you should aim for the lower end of the heart rate target zone.

Check your heart rate from time to time. Most fitness facilities post a table of appropriate heart rates; keep your rate at the low end of the range appropriate for your age.

Strength training

Building and maintaining muscle mass is an important part of any exercise program. But be cautious—avoid any weight training that involves holding your breath or straining. Get medical clearance before starting or continuing a weight training program.

Rules to exercise by

Aerobic exercise

Exercises using the large muscle groups include walking, swimming, stationary cycling, and low-impact aerobics.

Start slowly: take 15 minutes to warm up your muscles with gentle activity. Stretching or vigorous activity with "cold" muscles can give you unnecessary aches and pains or even injuries to muscles and ligaments.

Take rest breaks when you feel like it. Keep your heart rate at the low end of the target exercise heart rate for your age.

It is important to take 10 to 15 minutes to cool down, by working at less intensity until your heart rate returns to normal.

Drink plenty of water before, during, and after your exercise session.

Be careful when doing sports that require balance and coordination—your centre of gravity changes every day.

Avoid contact sports and activities that may cause you to fall or be hit, for example, downhill skiing, mountain climbing, floor hockey, water skiing, or soccer.

Strength training

Avoid any exercise that causes you to hold your breath and bear down at the same time, such as heavy weight-lifting routines.

Abdominal exercises should be changed to use only the side-lying or standing positions.

You should avoid over-stretching ligaments and tendons, which may be more flexible because of pregnancy hormones.

The most important muscles to tone now are the pelvic muscles. See page 34 for Kegel exercises.

At the gym or fitness centre

Avoid exercises that strain your lower back, and always practise good posture.

Avoid exercising in a warm and humid environment. Hot tubs, saunas, and steam rooms, for example, should be avoided (or limited) to prevent an increase in your baby's body temperature.

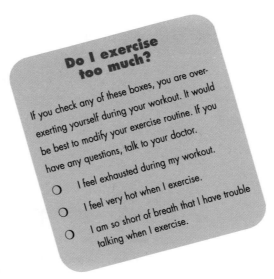

Do I exercise too much?

If you check any of these boxes, you are over-exerting yourself during your workout. It would be best to modify your exercise routine. If you have any questions, talk to your doctor.

O I feel exhausted during my workout.

O I feel very hot when I exercise.

O I am so short of breath that I have trouble talking when I exercise.

Kegel exercises strengthen your pelvic floor muscles

Doing Kegel exercises is strength training for the muscles that surround your pelvic floor, getting them ready for the delivery. You can do Kegels anywhere and any time, but aim for 12 to 20 repetitions at least three times a day. It's easy to learn.

This will help prevent urinary stress incontinence—"accidents" when you cough, lift, or laugh. Get used to the routine; it's a good habit for a lifetime, to help you get back in shape after childbirth or to help prevent incontinence problems later in life.

1 Relax
and sit or stand comfortably.

2 Find your pelvic muscle.
Imagine that you are trying to hold back urine, or a bowel movement. Squeeze the muscles you would use to do that.

3 Tighten the muscles for five to 10 seconds.
Do not hold your breath—breathe normally. Do not tighten your stomach or buttocks—keep them relaxed.

4 Now relax
the muscles for about 10 seconds.

5 Repeat
the cycle of squeeze - hold - relax 12 to 20 times.

Pelvic tilts may help to relieve your backache

This simple exercise done two or three times a day can help to strengthen your abdominal muscles and take some pressure off your aching back. Relax your back. Exhale and pull your buttocks forward, pulling your pubic bone upward and curving your spine. Hold this position for a count of three and inhale and relax. Repeat five times.

Chapter Three

Gentle growth: the second trimester

How does this baby measure up?

The bone you can feel above your pubic area is the pubic bone. The top curve of your uterus is the fundus. Your doctor or nurse may measure symphysis fundal height (SFH – the distance from your pubic bone to the top of your fundus) at each prenatal visit. This measurement is an indicator of the rate your baby is growing. The fundus usually reaches out of your pelvis by about the 12th week of pregnancy and reaches under your rib cage by the 36th week. Between the 18th and 30th week, the height of the fundus in centimetres is close to the age of the baby in weeks.

During this second trimester, your pregnancy is considered well established and the chance of having a miscarriage is much less. You will probably feel more like your old self once you leave the morning sickness and minor discomforts of the first trimester behind you. Many women enjoy this part of their pregnancy because they are comfortable with their size and they like the way they look. Your baby will be growing at a rapid pace and you will feel active movements from within your body as your baby rolls, somersaults, and kicks.

Your changing body

During your second trimester, the maturing placenta takes over most of the hormone production; your hormone levels will begin to even out, and you will probably feel more serene and settled.

You may worry if your friends or family comment that you seem small—or large—for your dates. But if you have been having regular prenatal visits, you know that your baby is growing at an acceptable rate. So why don't *you* look the right size?

Your body shape and size are related to many other factors than the baby's size. Your pre-pregnancy height, weight and build, and whether or not this is your first pregnancy, are all factors. Short women tend to look bigger, and large boned or taller women tend to look smaller. Second-time mothers tend to have bigger bellies because the abdominal and uterine muscles have been stretched.

The pigmentation of your skin may have changed, so that you have a brownish vertical line down the middle of your abdomen, called the *linea nigra*. Some women develop brownish, uneven marks around the eyes and over the nose and cheeks. This condition usually disappears when hormone levels return to normal after your baby's birth.

As your breasts prepare themselves for feeding your baby, you may notice a little leaking of colostrum from the nipples. Colostrum is the clear sticky fluid your breasts prepare for baby's first feedings, before your breast milk comes in. It contains many important antibodies to protect your baby against infections.

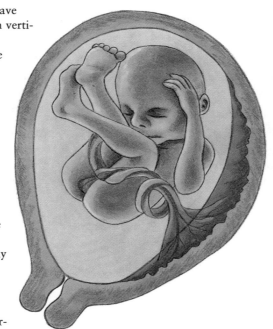

In preparation for the birth, hormones cause the ligaments and cartilage of your pelvis and back to soften.

Your developing baby

The baby really looks like a baby now; he's perfectly formed with all his body systems in place, functioning, and beginning to mature. The skin is red because the blood vessels are close to the surface. Some fat is starting to form under the skin, and a thick protective coating of a cheesy, whitish substance called vernix covers the entire body. The eyelids open and close by 26 weeks, the fingernails are full length and many babies have a visible hairline. Eyebrows and scalp hair become visible at the end of the 20th week; eyelashes can be seen at 24 weeks. The amniotic sac contains a large amount of fluid that is made up of nutrients for growth and the baby's urine. The umbilical cord is thick, strong, and very firm (which also helps prevent knots from forming).

Notes from your prenatal visits around 16 to 24 weeks

As at the last visit, your examination will include weighing and measuring you and your baby.

At about 16 to 18 weeks, your doctor may suggest a screening ultrasound test.

This test enables the doctor to measure the size of your baby to confirm the date your baby will be due.

At this visit, your doctor will also want to talk about any questions you may have about your changing body as you approach the halfway point in pregnancy. One of the biggest concerns you both will have is the possibility of a baby born too soon.

Recording your progress

Date:

Week of pregnancy:

Blood pressure:

Weight:

Fetal heart rate:

Premature labour

Not everyone understands how important it is to carry a baby to full term. Some women hope for a premature baby, thinking a small baby may be easier to deliver.

In fact, premature labour is one of the most common problems in pregnancy and it is the cause of 75 percent of all newborn deaths in babies born without birth defects. Premature babies are more delicate and can have life-long problems related to their prematurity. In general, the more premature a baby is, the more severe the problems. Babies born before the 25th week usually do not survive.

It is important to know early whether premature labour is occurring, as it sometimes can be stopped or delayed so there is time to give medicine that can help the baby, and treat conditions causing premature labour.

What causes premature labour?

Why some women develop premature labour, and others don't, is not well known. What we do know is that about half of all premature labours begin for unknown reasons to women who are perfectly healthy and whose pregnancies were otherwise normal. However, certain things seem to increase a woman's chances of going into early labour.

What you do during your pregnancy can help you carry your baby longer, and give him a better start. Research has shown that the more women know about the signs and risks of premature labour, the lower the rate of premature births.

In France, one long-term study showed a large reduction in overall prematurity rate when these things were done:

- There was public education about preterm labour and the importance of healthy full-term babies to society as a whole.

- Special seats on buses and special parking places were set aside for pregnant women.

- Pregnant women were encouraged to keep their own pregnancy record (much like this book).

Am I at risk to have premature labour?

Check all the boxes that apply to you.

- ○ No regular prenatal care.
- ○ High blood pressure.
- ○ Great deal of stress in my life.
- ○ Physical abuse from my partner or someone else.

- ○ Carrying more than one fetus.
- ○ A previous baby of mine was born too early.
- ○ Body weight less than 45.5 kg (100 pounds).
- ○ Chronic illness.
- ○ A smoker.

- ○ I quit smoking cigarettes, but not until after my 32nd week of pregnancy.
- ○ Work long hours (more than 8 a day) or shift work.
- ○ My work is physically strenuous.

If you checked one or more boxes, you are at risk to have premature labour and should talk to your doctor about precautions that may benefit you.

These are some of the risk factors for premature labour, and how the risk can be reduced:

Smoking.

It is best not to smoke during pregnancy. You can still benefit your baby if you quit smoking before you reach 32 weeks. Read the section on smoking on page 11.

Working too hard.

Working long hours, doing strenuous kinds of work and being tired all the time can lead to a preterm birth. Read the section about "strenuous work" on page 45.

Physical and emotional abuse.

When someone hurts you, they can also hurt your unborn baby. Even emotional abuse can lead to a preterm birth because your stress levels are so high. Please seek the help you need by calling a family crisis centre in your area.

Incompetent cervix - a rare condition in which the cervix dilates (opens) early and is associated with premature labour.

This can sometimes be diagnosed during a vaginal examination or by measuring the size of the cervix during an ultrasound. Sometimes this can be treated by sewing the cervix closed with a "drawstring" stitch and removing the sutures when the baby is full term.

Fibroids in and/or on your uterus can cause it to be misshapen.

If the fibroids are large enough to deform the uterus, and if they are detected before pregnancy, they may be removed. Small fibroids usually don't cause problems during pregnancy.

Bleeding during second trimester.

A small amount of bleeding can occur if the placenta begins to separate a bit from the lining of the uterus before labour starts. Each case of bleeding should be treated separately and may be treated differently depending on the cause. Always notify your doctor about bleeding.

Abdominal surgery during pregnancy.

Sometimes abdominal surgery is needed when a woman is pregnant (for example, for appendicitis). Surgery that is wanted but not essential (elective) should be avoided until after the baby is born.

Infection in the mother (most commonly vaginal, cervical, kidney, bladder infections).

You may have a bladder or kidney infection if you have pain when you urinate, if you have to go often, and if when you do only a small amount of urine comes out. You may have an infection in your vagina or cervix if you notice an unusual vaginal discharge, have pain in your pelvis or groin area, or a fever. Notify your doctor.

Premature labour can happen to anyone, but what you do can help prevent it. Learn the signs of premature labour, and act right away if you think you are in labour.

Call the hospital and talk to a nurse in the case room:

Phone: _____

Call your doctor:

Phone: _____

An underweight mother.

Treatment depends on the cause of the problem. Sometimes this problem is helped by eating healthy, good food on a regular basis. Talk to a registered dietitian if you are underweight and having problems.

Placenta previa - a condition in which the placenta implanted and grew over the opening of the cervix (where the baby must come out). This can lead to hemorrhaging during labour.

This problem is usually found during routine ultrasound testing. The mother is often confined to bed for the last few weeks of pregnancy and the baby is usually delivered by caesarean section before labour has a chance to begin.

Premature rupture of membranes - the sac of amniotic fluid breaks or leaks before your baby reaches full term.

Some studies link this to infections in the uterus, but further research needs to be done. If your membranes rupture early, treatment depends on how much amniotic fluid is lost and how close to your due date you are. Notify your doctor.

Gestational hypertension (high blood pressure caused by pregnancy) is treatable in various ways depending on the severity. Read more about this on page 52.

Chronic illness in the mother.

Some illnesses (diabetes, high blood pressure) may become out of control during the pregnancy and in some situations the only way to stop the worsening condition is to deliver the baby. Sometimes the labour will begin too early on its own, and in other cases, the labour needs to be brought on (induced).

Signs of problems in pregnancy

Bleeding.

An excessive discharge of clear or semi-clear watery fluid from your vagina.

Unexplained abdominal pain.

A decrease in the amount your baby moves inside you.

Your baby is not moving inside you.

Regular contractions of the uterus before your baby is due.

Unusual and constant headaches.

Blurred vision or spots before your eyes.

Dizziness.

Extreme tiredness.

Premature babies

About seven of every 100 babies will be born premature, which means they are born too early, before they reach full term. Normally, labour begins sometime after your 37th week of pregnancy and before the end of your 41st week. If labour starts before you reach your 37th week, your labour is considered early or premature.

The earlier a baby is born, the more problems he may face just to survive. The main reason these babies have problems is that their body organs are not ready to work all by themselves. These are called immature body systems. For example, a baby's lungs may not be fully able to take over the baby's breathing until close to the end of the pregnancy. Lungs that are not "ready" before the baby is born can result in mild to severe breathing problems for the newborn that may last a lifetime. An immature stomach and bowel can lead to feeding problems. When the immune system that protects your baby from catching certain diseases is not able to work on its own, your baby is more likely to get infections.

Premature babies can develop problems with their eyes and ears. They are redder and thinner than full-term babies because the blood vessels are so close to the skin surface and they have very little fat under their skin. Without fat deposits, premature babies have problems staying warm. Under the abnormal circumstances of premature labour, they are also more likely to be delivered by caesarean section. As an expectant mother, it is by far in your best interest, and in the best interest of your unborn child, to do all that you can to prevent your child from being born before he reaches full term.

Your baby's lung maturity

Your baby's lungs do not begin to produce enough of a very important substance called surfactant until some time after the 32nd week. Surfactant coats the inner walls of the air sacs to protect these sacs from sticking together when your baby takes his first breath. Babies born without this protective coating of surfactant are likely to develop a condition known as respiratory distress syndrome (RDS). This syndrome can also lead to a variety of other problems for the newborn. Some of these premature babies may need intensive care monitoring including the use of a life-supporting respirator to help them breathe or to breathe for them.

Doctors sometimes choose to test your amniotic fluid while you are in premature labour (although this is not always necessary) to help them determine if your baby has enough surfactant to prevent RDS from developing. Under some circumstances, giving the mother a steroid injection just before her baby is born can quicken fetal lung maturity.

Checking for premature labour

Labour begins when your uterus begins to contract at regular intervals. In addition, to prepare for the descent of your baby down the birth canal, the cervix will begin to thin out (efface) and open up (dilate). The protective mucous plug that formed at the entrance of your uterus during pregnancy may dislodge to produce a bloody, mucous show. Your waters may break, that is, the sac filled with amniotic fluid that surrounds your baby may suddenly rupture.

The only way to know for sure if you are in premature labour is to be checked by a nurse/midwife or doctor to determine what the contractions are like and if the cervix is opening. At that time, the doctor or nurse will check your baby's heart rate and an ultrasound may be done to confirm the size, age, and position of your baby.

If your labour has been confirmed as real labour (not false labour), and depending on how close to full term you are, you and your doctor will need to make a decision to try to stop your labour or to let the labour progress. Efforts to give your baby more time to mature inside your uterus are usually beneficial to your baby.

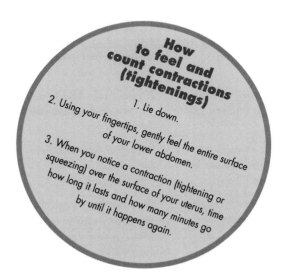

How to feel and count contractions (tightenings)

1. Lie down.

2. Using your fingertips, gently feel the entire surface of your lower abdomen.

3. When you notice a contraction (tightening or squeezing) over the surface of your uterus, time how long it lasts and how many minutes go by until it happens again.

What to do if you suspect you are in premature labour.

 Stop whatever activity you are doing and rest.

 Call the labour and delivery ward where you are planning to deliver your baby and describe your symptoms to an obstetrical (maternity) nurse.

 Go immediately to the nearest emergency room if:

• your water breaks

• you are bleeding

• you are in pain

• you are having regular contractions that are coming closer together and getting stronger.

What you can do to prevent premature labour

There are other basic things which you can do in an effort to try to prevent your baby from being born too soon.

Quit smoking
Try to understand why you smoke, and seek help to learn other ways of dealing with these issues. Ask around in your community about "Quit Smoking" programs. Ask your doctor about programs to help you quit.

Eat properly
Talk to a registered dietitian about your eating habits. Plan your meals around the basic food groups and avoid junk food. Drink plenty of milk.

Get help if you need it
You have a right to feel safe. If you are being abused, call your local women's shelter and ask where you can go for help.

Get plenty of rest
Plan ahead to be sure a certain part of your day will be set aside for you to rest. Don't feel guilty for resting. It is very important during pregnancy.

Learn ways to reduce stress
Talk to people you trust about how you feel. Learn relaxation techniques such as meditation and self-massage to reduce your stress. Consider yoga.

Avoid strenuous work
Read what is considered strenuous work on page 45, and try hard not to do these things during pregnancy.

Avoid overexertion when exercising during pregnancy
Even though you are physically fit, it is important not to increase your work-out intensity during certain times of your pregnancy. Read more about this on pages 31-33.

Learn to recognize the signs of premature labour
Prenatal classes through your hospital or community are an excellent way to learn. Read about the signs of premature labour on page 43. Talk to your doctor.

Learn the steps to take if you think you are in premature labour.
Talk to your doctor about what you should do. Write down the phone numbers to call and what your doctor wants you to do if you go into premature labour (see instructions on page 43).

Visit your doctor regularly during pregnancy
This is one of the most important things you can do to prevent premature labour because it gives your doctor a chance to find or prevent problems which may cause your baby to be born early.

Gestational diabetes

For some women, the pregnancy hormones change the way their bodies use insulin, and they go on to develop a type of diabetes because of the pregnancy. This is called gestational diabetes. Most will develop uncomplicated gestational diabetes, which means they will be able to control their blood sugar levels by eating a special diet and exercising. A small percentage may require insulin by injection to control their blood sugar levels. For most, the condition disappears after the baby is born, but some may go on to develop diabetes later in life. With preparation, good control, and professional care, most women with gestational diabetes have a safe pregnancy and a healthy baby.

(For a discussion on the special requirements of women who have Type 1 or insulin-dependent diabetes at the time they become pregnant, see page 29.)

About fetal movement

A baby moves her arms and legs as a form of exercise and to change her position to be more comfortable. If you are pregnant for the first time, you may not feel your baby move until you are in about your 19th week. If this is a second (or later) child, you will usually feel movement sooner, around the 17th week. From that point on, you should feel your baby move at different times of the day, every day. Keep in mind, a baby will have sleep periods throughout the day, and will have other times when she is more active. You may be asked to keep track of your baby's movements by counting the number of kicks you feel.

About work

In normal, uncomplicated pregnancies, the type of work you do is not usually a problem. However, strenuous work or prolonged standing have been shown in some studies to be linked to a slight rise in such problems as low-birth-weight babies, premature labour, and miscarriage. To find out if your work is considered too strenuous, answer the questions in the box on this page.

Is my work strenuous work?

Check any of the following boxes that apply to your job.

- ○ stoop or bend over more than 10 times per hour.
- ○ climb a ladder more than three times in an eight-hour shift.
- ○ stand for more than four hours at one time.
- ○ climb stairs more than three times per shift.
- ○ work more than 40 hours per week.
- ○ work shift work.
- ○ will be expected to lift more than 23 kg (50 lbs) after the 20th week of my pregnancy.
- ○ will be expected to stand for more than four hours and lift more than 11 kg (24 lbs) after 24 weeks.
- ○ will be expected to stoop, bend or climb ladders after my 28th week.
- ○ will be expected to lift heavy items after my 30th week.
- ○ will be expected to stand still more than 30 minutes of every hour after 32 weeks.

If you checked any of the above boxes, the work may be considered too strenuous to do during your pregnancy. Your doctor may recommend that you change the work you do until after your baby is born. Read more about work during pregnancy on page 7.

Common discomforts in the second trimester

Backaches

Your growing abdomen causes you to lean back to adjust your centre of gravity, which puts your back muscles under constant strain. In addition, the weight of the uterus in your pelvis, in combination with joint movement and softening, can also give you backaches during pregnancy. To prevent backaches, always try to sit up straight, avoid wearing high heels, lift using your leg muscles and not your back muscles (or resist lifting altogether), and avoid standing for long periods of time. Applying heat to your aching back or asking your partner for a back massage may help. Yoga, stretching, and relaxation techniques may prove beneficial and are worth investigating. Read about pelvic tilt exercises on page 34 that may help to relieve back strain. Be sure to change your body positions often and take time out of your busy day to lie down, put your feet up and relax.

Constipation

During pregnancy, food movement through the bowel can become slower. This slowing-down process can lead to constipation. In addition (and aside from turning your stools black), iron supplements can also cause constipation. To help keep the stool from becoming dry and hardened, it is recommended that you drink at least eight glasses of fluid (juice, water, milk) daily.

Getting regular exercise and eating plenty of raw fruits, vegetables, and fibre will also help to move food through your intestine. Your doctor may suggest taking a bulk-forming agent or stool softener.

Hemorrhoids

Many expectant mothers will develop hemorrhoids—a varicose vein of the rectum. Hemorrhoids often flare up during pregnancy because of the additional pressure your growing uterus places on the veins. If a woman strains to have a bowel movement because the stool is hard, the hemorrhoids become worse, and may push out around the anal opening. Sometimes they are painful and bleed. Try to avoid constipation with a diet high in fibre, fruits, vegetables, and grains. Drink plenty of fluids to help keep your stool soft. Your doctor may suggest ointments to help shrink the hemorrhoids.

Urinary tract infections (UTI)

The urinary tract involves the kidneys, ureters, bladder, and urethra. Infections in the urinary tract are common during pregnancy. Urine is made in the two kidneys. From each kidney, urine drips down tubes (ureters) into the bladder. When the bladder is full, urine exits the body through one tube called the urethra. Infections of this body system can sometimes be hard to detect. The common signs of an infection in your lower urinary tract (bladder) are: pain when you urinate, urinating unusually often, and only urinating a very small amount even though you felt a great urgency to go. This condition is easily treatable with antibiotics. An upper-urinary tract infection (involving the kidneys) is more serious. It can cause chills, fever, nausea, vomiting, backache, pain in the side, and lower abdominal discomfort. Women who are prone to urinary tract infections should be especially careful. UTIs are thought to be one of the main causes of premature labour. Be sure to inform your doctor about flu-like symptoms during pregnancy because it may be something more serious.

Indigestion and heartburn

If you feel a burning sensation at the back of your throat, lower in your food pipe (esophagus), or in your stomach, you may be suffering from indigestion related to pregnancy hormones and the pressure of a growing uterus.

It sometimes helps to eat and drink smaller amounts at one time, but you will need to eat and drink more often. Avoid caffeine and greasy, spicy foods that are known to cause gas. Sit upright after a meal to allow time for the food to pass from the stomach into the intestine. It is safe to take antacids. If these methods don't help, speak to your doctor.

Groin pain

The round ligament that holds the uterus in place sometimes goes into spasms when it stretches as your baby grows. This stretching feels like a stabbing pain on one or both sides of your lower abdomen, or it can feel like a dull ache. These pains seem to be most common in the second trimester. Pregnant women sometimes worry these pains are premature labour pains. It may help to avoid turning your waist quickly and when you do feel pain, lean into it (bend toward the pain) to help relax the tension on the muscles. Lie down and get some rest and of course, if the pain persists or becomes worse, and if changing positions does not relieve it, get checked either in the obstetrical ward of your hospital or your doctor's office.

Dizziness if you lie flat on your back

One of the largest blood vessels in your body, called the *vena cava*, transports blood from the lower part of your body back to your heart. It lies beside your spine. If your heavy uterus compresses the vena cava against your spine, the blood supply to your heart, lungs, and brain can be reduced. You may feel lightheaded and dizzy. This condition can also reduce your baby's blood supply. For this reason, it is important not to lie flat on your back during the last few months of pregnancy. Although lying on either side is fine, lying on your left side whenever possible is the best position to improve blood flow through the vena cava.

Swelling of legs, ankles, and feet

A small amount of swelling in your legs and ankles is normal during pregnancy. This type of swelling builds up each day and should all but disappear by the time you get up the next morning. It can be more of a problem if the weather is quite warm. Swelling of the hands or face may mean you have a different, more serious problem. Read about gestational hypertension on page 52.

Stretch marks

For some women, reddish streaks, commonly referred to as stretch marks, develop over their breasts, abdomen, and thighs during pregnancy. There has been no study done to our knowledge that says whether or not applying lotions and oils to your abdomen will reduce stretch marks. That being said, many women apply oil (particularly Vitamin E oil or lanolin) to their abdomen. Whether or not this helps with stretch marks is unknown. Regardless, the rhythmic motion of rubbing your belly with lotions and oils will be relaxing for both you and your unborn child and it certainly can't do any harm.

Dry, itchy skin

Avoid the use of soaps (if you must use soap, try glycerine soap) because they tend to wash away the natural lubricants in your skin. Lying in a tub of water for too long can also dry out your skin by washing away natural oils. Putting oil or a soothing skin softener like Aveeno® in the bath will help. If you use bath oil, take care getting out of the tub, which may become slippery. After a bath or shower, apply body lotion to damp skin to help keep your skin supple, soft, and moisturized.

Tips to help reduce the swelling in your legs and feet:

- Get regular exercise using your legs (swimming, walking).
- Avoid crossing your legs.
- Wear support hose and avoid socks with tight bands of elastic around the top.
- Don't stand for long periods of time.
- Raise your legs above the level of your heart whenever you can.

Chapter Four

Home stretch:
the third trimester

As you near the end of your pregnancy, you will probably begin to feel a bit anxious and tired, and will be looking forward to having the baby. During your last month of pregnancy, your prenatal visits will be more frequent, as often as once every week for the last month. Your blood pressure, urine, and the position of the baby will be checked at each visit.

Most women go into labour some time after their 38th week and before the end of their 41st week of pregnancy.

Your changing body

During your third trimester, you are visibly pregnant. The top of the uterus will grow from above the navel to under the rib cage and your abdomen will increasingly protrude. You may feel increasing discomfort from this, feeling pressure on your ribs, stretching of the abdominal muscles, and pressure in the pelvis. You may feel sharp pains in the groin or vagina, as your baby's head goes into the pelvis.

Your developing baby

Your baby is fully formed and growing steadily from 25-26 weeks, when his weight will be 700-900 grams (1 1/2 to 2 pounds). By 35-36 weeks, he will weigh 2500 grams (5 1/2 pounds). By the time he is ready to be born, he will weigh between 3000 and 4000 grams (6 1/2 to 9 pounds).

Although all the organ systems are there, they are still growing and maturing. The baby's arms and legs are bent close to his body. He has periods of activity and rest (like a newborn does). Breathing movements become regular at 20-21 weeks. Your baby's lungs become capable of breathing air at between 26-29 weeks. The baby is beginning to feel crowded inside the uterus, but you should still feel active movement every day.

A good volume of amniotic fluid surrounds and protects him.

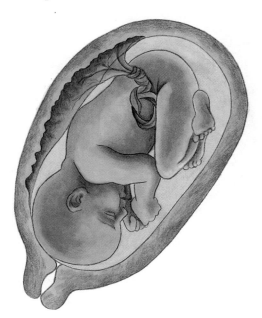

Notes from your prenatal visits from 24 to 32 weeks

Your examination will include weighing and measuring you and your baby. As at your last visit, signs of premature labour will be discussed, as well as how you are getting along with minimizing the risks. Are you continuing to eat well and get regular exercise? Are you protecting your baby from cigarette smoke and alcohol? Are the conditions at work stressful or physically tiring? Do you get enough rest?

If you have had any tests or a screening ultrasound since your last office visit, the results will be reviewed with you.

As at other visits, your plans for the big day and what you can expect will be reviewed. These discussions and your reading will help you get a clear picture of the choices you have for birthing your baby, and you will begin to develop opinions about what you think is best for you, your baby, your partner, and your family.

Breastfeeding is another big topic at this visit (see pages 53-55).

Recording your progress

Date:

Week of pregnancy:

Blood pressure:

Weight:

Fetal heart rate:

Am I at risk of getting gestational hypertension?

Check the boxes that apply to you.

- ○ My first pregnancy
- ○ High blood pressure before I got pregnant
- ○ Have diabetes
- ○ Have medical condition which causes my kidneys not to work properly
- ○ Carrying more than one baby
- ○ Very low income
- ○ Younger than 18
- ○ Older than 35

If you checked any boxes, you are at risk of developing gestational hypertension.

Gestational hypertension (toxemia)

Expectant mothers who develop high blood pressure because they are pregnant are said to have the condition known as gestational hypertension. This condition is also known as toxemia or as pre-eclampsia. Hypertension is the medical term for high blood pressure.

When a woman has gestational hypertension, her blood vessels constrict, which may reduce the blood supply to her placenta. This, in turn, may reduce the blood supply to her baby and slow the baby's growth. In addition to the high blood pressure, this condition often causes excess protein to spill over into the urine, and often, swelling of the face, hands, feet, and ankles.

Signs of gestational hypertension (toxemia)

If you have any of these symptoms, call your doctor right away.

Pain in the upper right part of the abdomen.

Constant, severe, or changing **headaches.**

Spots in front of your eyes and/or **blurred vision**

Unusual swelling, particularly around the face, and weight gains that are sudden and more than one pound per day.

Your doctor will check for high blood pressure (greater than 140/90) and protein in your urine.

Who will develop it?

About seven of every 100 expectant mothers will develop gestational hypertension. Most of them will be first-time mothers. Women who had high blood pressure before getting pregnant are also more likely to develop the condition.

Treatment for gestational hypertension

If you are diagnosed with gestational hypertension, every attempt will be made by your health care team to allow your baby to remain in the uterus for as long as possible—provided this doesn't cause an increased risk to you or your baby.

In a mild form of the condition, bed rest is usually enough to bring down the slightly high blood pressure. When resting, you will be asked to lie on your sides (never on your back) to improve the blood supply to your uterus and kidneys. In some situations, your doctor may recommend that you be hospitalized until your blood pressure is under control, and/or you may be given medication to help lower your blood pressure.

Severe gestational hypertension results in extremely high blood pressure and can cause problems in the mother's kidneys, liver, and brain. Seizures can happen because of changes in the brain. Untreated and severe gestational hypertension can lead to the death of the mother and her baby, although this is very rare today. Drugs will be given in an attempt to lower the mother's blood pressure and to prevent seizures. When this condition is severe, the best thing to do is to deliver the baby.

Feeding your baby

Over the past 20 years, breastfeeding has been studied a great deal. Researchers have identified many clear benefits for both the mother and the child. Based on this scientific evidence, the Society of Obstetricians and Gynaecologists of Canada (SOGC), the Canadian Paediatric Society, the World Health Organization (WHO), and the United Nation's Children's Fund (UNICEF) agree that the best food source for the first six months of life is breast milk.

Why breast is best

Women have always breastfed their children and breastfeeding is still the ideal way to feed children. Today, 75 percent of Canadian women having babies will breastfeed. As a nursing mother, you will receive emotional and practical support from many sources.

Breast milk, including the colostrum, contains antibodies that boost your baby's immune system and help fight disease. This stronger immune system lowers the chance of your baby getting an infection. A few examples of infections are colds, ear infections, stomach flus, baby measles, kidney infections, pneumonia, and meningitis. Breastfed babies have a lower chance of some bowel disorders (e.g., celiac disease, Crohn's disease), asthma, allergies, and eczema. Breast milk even lowers the chances of appendicitis. Breast milk is more easily absorbed and quicker to digest than formula, so breastfed babies tend to have fewer problems with constipation and stomach upset. Babies are hardly ever allergic to breast milk, but can have mild to severe allergic reactions to formula.

Only breast milk contains Omega 3 fatty acids, which are very important for brain development. Breast milk also has hormonally active proteins that are important in the development of your baby's gut, nerves, and disease-fighting cells.

Breastfeeding is also great for you. Breastfeeding triggers the release of certain hormones that will help your uterus return to its normal size. Breastfeeding also helps to protect you from breast, ovarian, and uterine cancer. Breastfeeding encourages closeness and a special bond between you and your baby. Finally, breastfeeding is free and involves no preparation. Formula feeding will cost $1500 or more during the first year.

If you are considering bottle-feeding, learn as much as you can about both methods. Consider your feelings, your partner's feelings, your cultural beliefs, nutrition, and cost.

Talk to other women and to such organizations as the La Leche League Canada Breastfeeding Referral Service (1-800-665-4324) or your local public health nurse for more information. In some areas, breastfeeding clinics and private breastfeeding experts, called lactation consultants, are also available to help you.

If you do decide not to breastfeed, your health care providers will respect your decision and support you.

Breastfeeding— getting started with colostrum

Most babies are ready to nurse within the first hour. Until your white milk comes in (usually 2–4 days after the birth), your breasts will produce a yellow, milk-like substance called colostrum. This colostrum contains antibodies, Omega 3 fatty acids, and the perfect balance of nutrients, minerals, vitamins, and trace elements for your baby. Your baby will be born with extra water stores and fat to use until your white milk comes in. In the meantime, the colostrum feedings are perfect for baby and all she needs. Some babies can lose weight after birth because they use up these fat and water stores. This weight loss should not be more than five percent of their birth weight. It is best to breastfeed your newborn whenever he or she seems hungry. Babies should not receive water supplements.

Myths about breastfeeding

1. **Breastfeeding is easy, natural, and instinctual.**

   False It is normal for many mothers and babies to have problems at first and need coaching.

2. **Every woman can produce enough milk to feed her baby.**

   False Almost every woman can produce enough milk to feed her baby.

3. **Babies must suck differently from a bottle than from a breast.**

   True Bottle feeding requires a different type of sucking than breastfeeding, so the baby may become confused at the difference between your nipple and a bottle's.

4. **If I breastfeed, my breasts will be more likely to sag afterward.**

   False Your breasts may look a bit different after breastfeeding but most changes in breast tissue (such as sagging) happen over time and are due to the aging process.

5. **If I breastfeed, I shouldn't bottle feed at all.**

   False Mothers can use a combination of breast and bottle feedings, although in the early months it is best to only breastfeed.

6. **Children should be weaned at six months of age.**

   False Breast milk is the best milk for the baby and toddler. The World Health Organization (WHO) recommends breastfeeding for two years or more. If breastfeeding is working well for you, there is no reason to quit before your child does so on his or her own. This is called infant-led weaning.

7. **Some mothers should not breastfeed.**

   True Very rarely, women have to take medication that can harm the baby. Women who are HIV-positive or who are abusing street drugs and alcohol should not breastfeed.

8. **Women with breast implants cannot breastfeed.**

   False Many women with implants can breastfeed. Implants are made of silicone, which is the same material found in many pacifiers and bottle nipples.

9. **Some women produce "blue" milk or watery milk which has no nutritional value.**

   False Breast milk may appear thinner than formula, but it is just as nutritious.

10. **If I am going to breastfeed, I should "prepare" my nipples by rubbing them with cream and "toughen" them by rubbing them with a rough cloth daily, for at least three months before my baby is born.**

    False The breasts secrete an oily substance on their own to keep nipples supple. Rubbing them with a rough cloth may cause skin damage.

11. **If I am going to breastfeed I should express colostrum to get it flowing before the baby is born.**

    False This is not necessary.

12. **Breastfed babies should be given a soother (pacifier) to help them learn to suck.**

    False Pacifiers may teach your baby poor sucking technique, hide his or her hunger signs, and are one way that disease is spread.

13. It is best to breastfeed a baby whenever he or she seems hungry.

True *Breastfeeding your baby on demand makes for a more satisfied baby. In the beginning, babies usually nurse 8 - 12 times a day.*

14. Both breastfed and bottle-fed babies need water supplements.

False *Feeding your baby water by bottle can lead to a reduced appetite at feeding time and it has no nutritional value.*

15. If I am going to breastfeed, I will have to be very careful to eat properly.

False *Mother's milk is of excellent quality unless a woman is on an extreme diet.*

16. I have to wean before I go back to work.

False *Mothers who return to work have a number of choices. Some mothers nurse when they are at home and express or pump their milk at work, for the baby to have the next day. Other mothers nurse when they are home and use frozen breast milk or formula when they are away.*

What is in baby formula?

Infant formulas provide your baby with the calories and nutrients he or she needs to grow. These formulas contain a variety of ingredients and they are listed on every label. Formulas are divided into two main groups: skimmed cows' milk based and soybean based. Oils such as coconut, sunflower, and soy are added, as are the essential minerals, vitamins, and trace elements needed for growth and development.

Still, no formula can come close to the milk a mother makes for her child; science cannot duplicate the complex mixture of protein, fats, hormones, and other products that are found in human breast milk.

In addition, no commercial formula on the market contains the white blood cells and antibodies that protect your baby from disease, and none contain the Omega 3 fatty acids that are important for brain development. Bottle-fed babies also tend to have more allergic responses to cows' milk formula than breastfed babies have to breast milk.

Recording your progress

Date:

Week of pregnancy:

Blood pressure:

Weight:

Fetal heart rate:

Recording your progress

Date:

Week of pregnancy:

Blood pressure:

Weight:

Fetal heart rate:

Recording your progress

Date:

Week of pregnancy:

Blood pressure:

Weight:

Fetal heart rate:

Your prenatal visits from 32 to 36 weeks

You will have prenatal visits every 2-3 weeks now. Your examinations will include weighing and measuring you and your baby. As at your last visits, your doctor will be looking for any signs of premature labour. Your baby and how she is growing will get a lot of the attention.

You and your doctor will review your birthing plan (pages 60-64) at this visit and talk about any concerns you may have about childbirth.

Group B streptococcus (GBS)

At about 36 weeks, you may be tested for the presence of the Group B streptococcus (GBS) bacteria. These are different from the bacteria that cause strep throat. If these bacteria are in your body but you don't have any signs of infection, you are said to be colonized (positive). The GBS bacteria are usually found in your vagina or rectum and can infect your bladder, kidneys, or uterus. Infections from GBS are usually not serious for the mother and are readily treated with antibiotics. However, if these bacteria are passed on to your baby during childbirth, there is a remote chance your baby could become infected, too. Babies who are infected with GBS may have mild to severe problems that may affect their blood, brain, lungs, and spinal cord.

Testing for group B strep

The most common way to test a woman for the presence of GBS bacteria is to swab her vagina and rectum with a Q-tip, which is then placed in special solution to see if the bacteria grow. This is called doing a "culture." Sometimes your doctor may also look for the presence of bacteria in your urine.

Treatment for group B strep

No method of testing and treating mothers infected with GBS prevents all cases of the GBS bacteria from being passed on to babies. It is very rare, but babies still die of GBS infection.

If you tested at 36 weeks as positive for GBS, you may be given antibiotics during labour. Some doctors do not routinely test for GBS, but instead treat women who are at a higher risk for developing GBS in the baby. Both approaches are acceptable.

You may be at higher risk to pass GBS on to your baby if you:

1. Start labour before you reach 37 weeks.

2. Reach full term, but your membranes have been ruptured more than 18 hours before your expected time of delivery.

3. Have an unexplained, mild fever.

4. Have already had a baby who had a GBS infection.

5. Have (or had) a bladder or kidney infection that was caused by the GBS bacteria.

What to expect in hospital

Obstetrical health care in Canada has changed—a lot—since your mother gave birth to you, and even more since her mother was "confined," as childbirth was once called.

Over the past 20 years or so, physicians, nurses, and mothers have promoted changes in the approach of obstetrical care. Family-centered maternity care has replaced the strict medical approach to care. Routine hospital practices were studied to be sure they were beneficial to women and some standard procedures such as enema and episiotomy were dropped from routine care.

Hospital obstetrical units have adapted to meet women's needs, by becoming warm and homelike places to have a baby, while offering excellent medical care when it is needed.

Care has been individualized, with women being encouraged to prepare a birthing plan to reflect their desires and options.

Birthing units and LDRP (labour, delivery, recovery, and postpartum) units were opened throughout Canada with help and guidance from obstetricians, family physicians, and nurses.

To improve the safety of childbirth for the mother and to make the event more enjoyable, most hospitals in Canada now promote the family-centered approach to maternity (obstetrical) care. When hospital maternity care programs include every member of the family, stronger and healthier families appear. Fathers and family tend to be more supportive when they feel needed and included in the childbirth process. Although it is usually best not to have young children present during labour and childbirth, it is recommended that they join their family as soon after the birth as possible to welcome the new family member.

The obstetrical nurse/midwife

The current trend in caring for normal pregnancies is to recognize the importance of the people who offer human support and understanding for the labouring woman. Many studies show that when an experienced obstetrical nurse or midwife closely helps a labouring woman, the risk of problems for the mother and the baby is less. Ideally, your labour and delivery nurse will also take care of you and your baby after the birth.

Childbirth is a normal life experience, not an illness

"Today, it should be possible for a woman with a low-risk pregnancy to go into the hospital, deliver normally and leave having had no intravenous, no medication, no enema, no shave prep and no blood tests during her stay."

The Society of Obstetricians & Gynaecologists of Canada (SOGC), 1997

Rooming in

In family-centered care, most babies "room in," staying in their mothers' hospital rooms and not in the newborn nursery. Under normal circumstances, it is healthy and best for mothers and their newborns to stay together in the same room from birth to discharge. In the past, the newborn nursery was considered cleaner, and therefore safer, for your baby than staying in the room with you, when in fact the opposite is true. When an infant stays in the same room as the mother, the mother does most of the handling. In the nursery, many different nurses, all of whom may be handling other infants, handle the infant. In spite of all the hand washing nurses do, the risk of infection for a newborn is greater in the nursery.

Family-centered care hospital checklist

My hospital:

○ **will accept the birthing plan** I have developed, or has a standard birthing plan I can adapt to suit my needs.

○ **will encourage me** to have a labour coach.

○ **offers the support of a professional** labour support person.

○ **encourages breastfeeding**, starting right after the birth.

○ **will not separate my baby** and me unless it is medically necessary.

○ **allows my baby to stay in my room** with me and my family.

○ **treats birth as a normal and natural process**, not an illness.

○ **will try to assign only one nurse** to me during my labour and delivery. (Some hospitals may not have enough staff to do this, but most will try.)

○ **accepts my individual religious beliefs** and wants to do all they can to accommodate my cultural needs.

○ **allows me the freedom of choice** with regard to procedures, labour positions, delivery positions, and pain control.

○ **has flexible visiting hours** and children are encouraged to visit early after the birth and as often as they want to.

If you checked most of these boxes, your hospital offers a family-centered approach to maternity care. If not, then most health care workers will still try very hard to meet your needs. You may find that by giving the staff your completed birthing plan, you may still be able to achieve the birth you desire.

Writing your birthing plan

A birthing plan is a written document that tells your doctor and the hospital staff what kind of childbirth you would like and how you would like your baby cared for after he is born.

How to write a birthing plan

A birthing plan should be simple and less than one page long. Try to be realistic in your requests and to keep in mind that your childbirth experience will include your health care team, yourself, your partner, the baby, and your family. Your birth plan will be most effective if you write down what you want to happen, and your preferences if what you want to happen isn't going to happen. For example, you may write, "I would prefer not to have an IV in place throughout labour, but only if and when it is needed."

When to write a birthing plan

Usually, a birthing plan is written after you talk over your childbirth plans with your doctor and once you know what your hospital offers in terms of routines and care. It is also a good idea to talk it over with your partner and your family if they are going to be involved in some way. However, it is your body, and your family needs to understand that you are the only one who can make some of the more personal decisions (for example, about pain control). Make two copies and give one to your doctor and one to the hospital staff before the end of your eighth month or as you enter the hospital in early labour.

Try not to be too detailed or complicated. No one can predict how your labour and birth will progress, so it is important that your birthing plan be flexible.

Things to think about in your birthing plan

We have listed some of the common things women talk about in their birthing plans. You don't have to mention all of them in your own birthing plan. If something is not as important to you, you can leave it out. If you think of something else that is not on this list, feel free to include it in your birthing plan.

The labour coach

Studies show that when a labouring woman is continuously supported by someone who cares for her (a labour coach), she will have a more positive experience. The hospital will provide you with a professional labour support partner (maternity nurse) who will help you during labour, delivery, and after the baby is born.

Enema

Hospitals today do not routinely give enemas. However, some women find that having an enema relieves pressure in the lower bowel, particularly if they had been constipated before labour.

Shave preps

Most hospitals today do not routinely shave the pubic area. Sometimes, if stitches are needed after an episiotomy, it is best to shave a tiny part of the area to help with putting in stitches.

Intravenous line (IV)

Unless your pregnancy is considered a high-risk pregnancy, or unless there is a medical reason, most hospitals do not start routine IVs. An IV provides access to your blood stream quickly in case of an emergency. Sometimes an IV is the best way to give you certain medications, such as antibiotics, labour-starting drugs, or as required for an epidural. Some women benefit from the extra IV fluids if they become dehydrated during labour.

Blood tests

Usually routine blood tests are not done if a pregnancy is considered low risk and normal. Sometimes, certain blood tests are needed (for example "blood sugar tests" if you are a diabetic) to make sure everything is going along well.

Inducing labour

If your labour has not started by the end of your 41st week, or if there are other medical complications, your doctor may consider inducing labour. Labour should not be induced without good reason. Read the section about overdue babies on page 69.

Monitoring the fetus

Evidence shows that during normal labour it is best to monitor the baby at regular intervals using methods that do not limit your movements. Under special circumstances, it will be necessary to monitor the baby using continuous fetal monitors (see page 75).

Movement during labour

Most hospitals today encourage mothers to move about freely during the early stages of labour. Evidence shows that this mild form of exercise in the early stages of labour helps labour to move along more quickly.

Eating and drinking during labour

In the very early stages of labour, eating and drinking small amounts may prevent dehydration and help keep your strength up. However, when you are in active labour, most women do not feel like eating, but may wish to have small amounts of clear fluids. In some high risk circumstances, food and drink may be restricted.

Pain relief

There are many different ways to help you cope with the pain of labour and childbirth, ranging from special breathing to an epidural block. When a labouring mother's pain is under control, she is better able to help with the birth. It is okay to choose natural childbirth (no pain killers) but it is also okay to change your mind if the pain becomes unbearable. Read more about ways to make labour easier in Chapter 6.

Pushing

At the end of active labour, the urge to push your baby out is strong; suddenly you will want to bear down (push). The body naturally wants to bear down a few short times during each contraction, and take breaths in and out between pushes. Evidence shows this method gives the baby the most oxygen. Sometimes a different method is encouraged in hospitals. Mothers may be encouraged to take a deep breath and hold it, then push one hard, long push with a deep breath at the end. Evidence shows this method may lower the baby's oxygen levels over time, but may speed up the delivery. Sometimes, the cervix is not quite ready for the baby to move through, and you may be instructed not to push. If that happens, you will be told what you can do to avoid pushing (such as a knee-to-chest position or special breathing).

Delivery positions

There is clear evidence today that sitting upright or semi-sitting for delivery is best. These positions seem to lower the time it takes to push a baby out. Lying on your side is also a natural delivery position which has many benefits. Squatting down can be beneficial because it improves the angle of the pelvis, to give the baby more room to come out, and the force of gravity enables the baby to slide out more quickly. Today, women's legs are no longer strapped into stirrups.

Episiotomy

There is no evidence to support routine episiotomy (making an incision or cut to widen the vaginal opening). There are more benefits to avoiding episiotomies, such as less pain after the baby is born, better sexual function later, and less relaxation of the pelvic muscles. Sometimes, an episiotomy is necessary to relieve pressure or to deliver a baby in distress more quickly.

Religious or cultural beliefs

Feel free to list your needs in this area, for example, traditions, beliefs, and expectations for yourself, the baby, and your family.

Rooming in

Studies show it is best for you and your baby to stay and sleep in the same room together. Babies who room in are handled mostly by their mothers. Babies in the nursery are handled by many people. Therefore, the risk of infection for a baby is greater in the nursery. Rooming in is a good opportunity for you and your baby to bond with each other.

Caesarean birth

If you know you are having a c-section, you may want to think about want kind of pain relief you want, or if you want your partner to attend. If you were to be faced with an emergency delivery, what would your choices be?

Breastfeeding

Starting to breastfeed

Evidence shows the best time to begin breastfeeding is within the first one to two hours, when the baby is most alert. This is also the perfect time to begin bonding with your baby.

Feeding schedules

Studies show it is best to breastfeed your baby whenever your baby seems hungry and not on a regular schedule. This is called demand feeding.

Breastfeeding

Studies show that most breastfed babies do not need feedings of anything other than breast milk. Water feedings using a bottle tend to lessen the baby's appetite, and the two different nipples may confuse the baby.

Asking for help

There are many ways that you can find help for breastfeeding. Sometimes the help will be offered, and sometimes you may have to ask for it. In many areas there are home nursing programs, public health clinics, breastfeeding clinics, and professional lactation (breastfeeding) consultants.

Chapter Five

All ready to go

Important things to think about before labour begins

How are you getting to the hospital? Is your car reliable? Make a back-up plan.

How easily are you able to reach your labour support partner when you go into labour?

How far from the hospital are you? It is best to drive the distance and time it. Consider the road conditions and rush hour traffic possibilities when you do. Plan an alternative route in case of road obstructions.

Where are you supposed to park the car?

Do you need to preregister at the hospital or can you just show up?

Who will take care of your children at home?

Do you need someone to feed your pets for you while you are hospitalized?

Your changing body

Some time toward the end of pregnancy, most babies will settle into the head down, or the engaged, position. Some people also call this event the time when the baby "drops" or "lightening." It can be normal if this doesn't occur until just before labour starts. When your baby settles deep into your pelvis, the head will rest on top of your cervix. You will feel different and look as though you are carrying the baby much lower. The good news is that after the baby drops, some of the pressure on your ribs will be relieved and you will probably breathe a little more easily. Sometimes, however, this low and heavy weight can add to muscle strain and back-aches.

The uterus is starting to have "practice contractions" (Braxton Hicks contractions) that may or may not be painless and should be irregular. You may notice them, or you may not. Because of the pressure the uterus places on the blood vessels in your pelvis, the swelling in your feet and ankles may be more noticeable. But swelling of the face and hands may be a sign of a more serious problem. (Read about gestational hypertension on page 52.)

Your pelvic bones have loosened and may ache, especially at the back. You may notice your breasts leaking some colostrum, leaving a crusty film on your nipples (although many women do not produce colostrum before the baby is born). Your breasts may feel full and heavy and will need a good support bra for the months to come, particularly when you breastfeed. Your abdomen may become so stretched that your navel pushes out. The brown pigment of your skin can become very noticeable near the end of pregnancy.

Your developing baby at full term

A baby at full term is plump and rounded. She will measure 46-51 cm (18-20 inches) in length, and weigh between 3000 and 4000 grams (6 1/2 to 9 pounds.) Most of the cheesy vernix that protected the skin is gone now, and the bit that remains is slippery and will help during the birth process.

The baby's eyes are open when awake, and closed when sleeping. Her lungs are now producing surfactant that will help them prepare for the first breath. A full-term baby's immune system is still not mature. To counter-balance this problem, your baby will get antibodies from you via your placenta before she is born, and more from your breast milk (colostrum) after she is born. The placenta is now about 20 cm (8-10 inches) in diameter and about 2.5 cm (1 inch) thick.

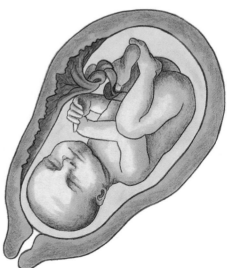

Your prenatal visits from 36 to 42 weeks

You will have prenatal examinations every week during the last 4-6 weeks. At each visit, you and your baby will be watched closely to make sure you and he are growing well and your body is continuing to prepare for the big event.

_____

_____

_____

_____

_____

_____

_____

_____

_____

_____

_____

_____

_____

_____

_____

_____

Recording your progress

Date: _____

Week of pregnancy: _____

Blood pressure: _____

Weight: _____

Fetal heart rate: _____

Recording your progress

Date: _____

Week of pregnancy: _____

Blood pressure: _____

Weight: _____

Fetal heart rate: _____

Recording your progress

Date: _____

Week of pregnancy: _____

Blood pressure: _____

Weight: _____

Fetal heart rate: _____

Packing your suitcase

It is best to pack your suitcase a few weeks before your due date, in case the baby arrives early. You may not have time to think about all the things to bring once labour starts.

A helpful checklist for you:

○ This book, pen, paper
○ Copy of your birthing plan
○ Housecoat, nightgown, and slippers
○ Loose-fitting clothes to go home in
○ Extra pair of socks
○ Bra (nursing or good support bra)
○ Underwear
○ Toothbrush, toothpaste
○ Hairbrush, comb
○ Camera, batteries, film
○ Change for phones and vending machines
○ Labour support items such as massage oil for back rubs

A helpful checklist for your baby:

○ Clothes to go home in
○ Diaper(s)
○ Receiving blanket
○ Warmer blanket
○ Hat
○ Car seat

Common discomforts in late pregnancy

Leg, calf, and foot cramps

Many women experience cramps during the last three months of pregnancy, mostly at night. These sudden cramps in the thighs, legs, calves, or feet can be very painful and are usually followed by an ache that lasts for a long time. When a cramp strikes, try this: in spite of the pain, point your toe toward your knee in an effort to stretch the muscle straight again. Then keep your foot in this flexed position while you slowly and carefully make circling movements with your lower leg. Afterward, deeply massage the cramped muscle to improve the blood supply to that area.

Difficulty sleeping

Having problems sleeping is common at any time throughout pregnancy, and most common in the last trimester. Your large abdomen makes finding a comfortable position a challenge, and the added trips to the bathroom at night don't help either. Try using a number of large pillows to prop up your legs, abdomen, and back (but do not lie flat on your back). Ask your partner for a back massage to help you drift off to sleep. It may help to take a warm bath before going to bed. Try keeping the bedroom temperature cool. Avoid sleeping pills; they can cross through the placenta and make your baby sleepy.

Vaginal discharge

The discharge from your vagina is normally greater during pregnancy, and it can become even more plentiful (even messy at times) during your last trimester. Wearing a sanitary mini pad may make you feel more comfortable and protected. This discharge should look and feel like the white of a raw egg. It should not be bloody (unless it is your mucous plug), watery (this could be amniotic fluid), or foul smelling (this may mean you have an infection). You should not have any pain, itching, or soreness in your vaginal area. Notify your doctor if you suspect a problem.

Pre-labour contractions

Labour is an action of the uterus that begins slowly and then gathers speed and strength. After months of stretching larger, the uterus will finally start to contract in the weeks before birth. These Braxton Hicks contractions are usually painless, and should be irregular. Many mothers are unaware of them when they happen.

Worries about labour

It is normal for you to have some worries about childbirth, especially if this is your first baby. In Canada, childbirth in a hospital setting is considered very safe and while it is true that things can go wrong, almost all babies are born normal and healthy. To return to the theme and purpose of this handbook, research has shown that being prepared and learning about the birth process will make a real difference. Women who have learned about labour and the birth process tend to be less frightened and anxious than women who have not. When there are fewer surprises, you will feel more confident and less anxious, and the pain will feel more manageable.

Overdue babies

About 10 percent of women will not have delivered their babies by the end of their 41st week, or within one week after their due date. When a pregnancy lasts beyond 41 weeks it is called post-term and the babies are said to be overdue. To be sure your pregnancy is truly post-term, your baby's due date must be accurate. Your due date should have been calculated early in your pregnancy using the dates of your last menstrual period and the results of the ultrasound that may have been done around your 16th to 20th week. Trying to calculate due dates late in pregnancy using uncertain menstrual dates or late ultrasounds is not reliable.

An aging placenta

A small percentage of overdue babies will develop health problems. We don't know why a few overdue babies have these problems, but it may be because of an aging placenta. As the placenta gets older, it deteriorates and can begin to lose its ability to do its job. When this happens it may mean fewer nutrients and less blood and oxygen will reach your baby and in some cases, this can cause your baby's growth to slow down.

Keeping your overdue baby safe

If your baby is still not born after your 41st week, or within a week after your due date, you and your doctor will face two choices—to monitor the baby closely, while awaiting the start of labour, or to induce labour. The "watch and wait" strategy is most often chosen if the cervix is "unripe" or not ready for labour.

There are several ways to monitor your overdue baby's health while you wait.

Counting the baby's movements—One of the best ways to determine if your overdue baby is active is to count the number of movements he makes. You can do "movement counts" at home any time of the day. You are the best judge of whether your baby is moving the same as he was before. Remember that overdue babies feel very crowded and their movements may not be as vigorous. But no matter what, you should still feel movement throughout the day, every day. You may be asked to write down your baby's movement counts.

Ultrasound testing—An ultrasound may be done to help doctors determine the health of your baby. The results of this test are often compared to any previous ultrasounds you may have had.

Non-stress test—A fetal heart rate recording, done at your doctor's clinic or at the hospital. The rate is measured for 20 to 30 minutes, and if the baby is healthy, the recording will show accelerations in the fetal heart rate and movement.

At an appropriate point, your labour may be started for you (induced).

True labour vs false labour

If you are in doubt about whether your labour is true or false, it may be helpful to time the contractions. Write down how many minutes apart they are, from the start of one contraction until the start of the next one, and note how long each one lasts. If possible, keep a record for one hour.

Strength of contractions

The contractions will get steadily stronger and you will be able to feel your uterus hardening.

The contractions do not get progressively stronger. They may weaken at times and even disappear for a while.

Effect of movement

If you move around, the contractions will still continue to get stronger and will not weaken or become further apart.

If you move around, the contractions will weaken, subside or stop for a time.

Regularity of contractions

The contractions usually become quite regular and predictable, usually beginning about five minutes apart (or less). They are usually between 30–70 seconds long.

The contractions never really settle down into a pattern. They are irregular.

true   false

Chapter Six

Your time is here

After months of waiting, and possibly when you least expect it, you will start to feel the beginning of labour and you will know the time to have your baby has finally arrived. Like most women, you may feel surprised, excited, and even a little scared.

When labour begins

It is believed that hormones play an important part in the start of labour, but no one knows for sure what really causes it. There is no way to predict exactly when your labour will begin.

Signs of labour

Some women realize they are in labour right away, others can't tell, and sometimes it is even hard for the experts to tell. If you are in doubt, you should go to the hospital.

Show—A mucous plug has formed at the opening of your cervix during your pregnancy. When the cervix begins to open, the plug is released. You may notice a thick, unusual discharge from your vagina that may be blood-tinged, or notice an increase in vaginal discharge that is clear or pinkish. This may happen several days before labour starts—wait for further signs.

Rupture of membranes—When the sac full of amniotic fluid that surrounds your baby springs a leak, or breaks completely, the membranes are said to be ruptured. This is often referred to as your "waters breaking." It can happen several hours before labour, or at any time during labour. Go to the hospital if this happens.

Contractions—Labour often begins with contractions of the uterus, as your uterus tightens and then relaxes. These contractions open the cervix and push the baby down the birth canal. See page 70 for a chart to help you tell the difference between true versus false labour.

Labour contractions are painful and regular, and usually last between 45 seconds and a minute.

When labour may be induced

An overdue baby is only one reason why labour may be induced. For example, if your water breaks without labour starting on its own, you will face a decision whether to wait for labour to start on its own or whether your doctor will induce your labour. Either course may be appropriate, depending on the situation. The decision may depend on such factors as how long the membranes have been ruptured, whether the cervix is ripe, the risk of infection, and your own feelings.

Also, it is best to induce a pregnancy at term (40 weeks) or before if the mother has high blood pressure that is worsening, an illness such as diabetes, signs that the baby is not growing well, or other medical concerns.

Usually, labour should be induced only for these valid medical reasons, and if it is induced for other "social" reasons, the baby should be at least full term, and the cervix should be ripe.

How labour is induced

There are several common ways to induce labour.

Stripping the membranes—The sac filled with amniotic fluid that surrounds your baby is attached to the inside of your cervix. It is a common and acceptable practice for your doctor to strip these membranes away from the cervix, without breaking through the membranes, in order to help ripen the cervix and prevent your pregnancy from being overdue. After discussions with you, your doctor will place a finger into your cervix (much like putting a finger into a small doughnut hole), and then circle the finger against the inside of the cervix to detach the membranes that are stuck to the sides. This routine and simple procedure is done in your doctor's office, with your consent, usually some time after 38 weeks. Most women experience a small amount of cramping that lasts a short time, along with a small amount of pinkish discharge.

Ripening the cervix—Normally, before labour starts, the cervix begins to soften, widen, and shorten. This is called ripening. If your cervix is not getting ready for labour on its own, and you are having labour induced, your doctor may try to ripen your cervix. This is commonly done by placing a special gel or tablet containing hormones (prostaglandin E_2) onto your cervix, or into your vagina. Another method is to place a rubber tube with a balloon on the end into the cervix. When the balloon is inflated inside the cervix, ripening may take place. It is very important to soften or ripen the cervix before inducing labour.

Rupturing the membranes—If the membranes of the amniotic sac are still unbroken, the next step may be to break them, using a simple and almost painless procedure. For most women, particularly if their cervix is ripe, labour will begin within 12 hours. Sometimes, even if your labour began on its own, this is done to help speed things up.

Starting the contractions—Your body naturally produces a hormone called oxytocin, which is responsible for starting uterine contractions. Medical researchers have developed drugs that are identical to the hormone your body naturally produces. These synthetic drugs can be given intravenously to start contractions. When the dose is increased, the contractions become more frequent and stronger.

Instructions for when labour begins:

The number I should call when labour begins is:

_____

_____

Calling this number will put me in touch with:

_____

_____

I should go directly to the hospital if:

_____

_____

Any special instructions I should follow when I am in labour are:

_____

_____

_____

73

Helpful tips for labour coaches

Judge the situation and try to fit in. If she is quiet, you can be quiet.

Some labouring women don't like to be touched during contractions and others need to be.

She may need a lot of words of encouragement, or very few.

If something you tried didn't work at one point during labour, try it again later. It may work then.

Always be positive and never criticize anything she does or wants.

When labour is very intense, some women say things they don't mean that may hurt your feelings. Try not to take it personally. It is the pain talking.

Keep the family updated by choosing one main person to call the others. Only this one person should call the hospital for information.

If the labour is long, make sure you get a bite to eat, so you don't feel faint during the delivery.

Labour support

Most women find it very comforting to have a familiar face around them during labour. You can choose anyone you wish to be your labour coach—including the baby's father, a friend, or a family member. Coaches can offer you the emotional support you need, rub your aching back if it helps, coach you to remember the special breathing you learned in prenatal classes, and hold your hand when you need it most. Some hospitals have volunteers to help labouring mothers.

A word about the labour coach's job

Studies show that women benefit in a number of ways if they have a supportive person who knows them to help them with their labour as a "coach."

As a labour coach, especially if this is your first time, you may be wondering what you can do to help during labour. Some coaches worry they may feel queasy, or not be able to offer enough support. But there are many things you can do to help your partner during labour.

Before labour begins, encourage your partner to rest often, and take over her share of the cleaning, laundry, and cooking.

If you were involved in the preparation of the birthing plan, you know what type of birth experience she hopes for. She may ask you to be her voice to the staff during her labour.

It is helpful for you to remain as calm as possible and to keep your movements slow, quiet, and steady when you are with her. Be encouraging and offer her words of praise. Help her to try to relax between contractions. When you assist with special breathing, allow her to follow her own rhythm (sometimes her body will tell her which rhythm is best and it may not be the pattern you learned and practised).

If she seems to lose control, remain close, talk her quietly through the contraction, keep eye contact, and try to get her back on track for the next one.

Be flexible about your birthing plan and don't feel upset if things don't go exactly the way you had planned. Listen carefully to your partner's wishes—they may change. Remember to take care of yourself during this long and stressful process. Take time to eat, drink, and rest.

Go to the hospital when:

Your water breaks in a gush or your water is leaking steadily.

Your contractions are regular and five minutes apart (and the hospital is less than 30 minutes away).

Your contractions are regular and 10 minutes apart (if the hospital is more than 30 minutes away).

If you are unsure, call the labour and delivery unit at your hospital.

Your labour and delivery nurse/midwife

If you have been under the care of a doctor and are planning to deliver your baby in hospital, you will meet your obstetrical nurse when you arrive at the hospital. Usually, labour and delivery professionals are registered nurses but some may have midwife qualifications. If possible, the same nurse will stay with you during your labour and delivery. In some provinces, licensed midwives also care for women during pregnancy, labour, and delivery.

Studies show that you will benefit in a number of ways by having a nurse or midwife who is focused on your care. These partners are there to help you master techniques to make your labour easier. They are also very experienced, and know when the birth is progressing normally and how to recognize when something is not going well.

The stages of labour

There are four stages of labour. The first stage begins when the contractions start and become regular, and ends when your cervix is fully dilated (10 centimetres). The second stage of labour begins when your cervix is fully dilated and ends when your baby is born. The third stage of labour begins after the baby is born and ends when the placenta is delivered. The fourth stage of labour ends about two hours after the birth. The average labour lasts about 12–14 hours for first-time mothers, while second and subsequent labours are generally shorter. Every labour is different and no one can predict what your labour will be like. These numbers are averages only. Your labour may be longer or shorter.

Monitoring your baby during labour

If your pregnancy is considered a normal one, as most are, studies show the best way to check your baby during labour is by listening to the fetal heart through the mother's abdomen. Ideally, your nurse will check the fetal heart rate (FHR) often and regularly by using a stethoscope or a hand-held Doppler, a machine that picks up the sounds of your baby's heart.

The heart rate will be checked for a full minute after a contraction, about two to four times every hour during the first stage of labour. When you begin the second stage of labour, and start pushing, your nurse may check the heartbeat every five minutes.

Sometimes a machine is used to read and record your baby's heartbeat and the length and strength of your contractions. This external monitor prints the information onto a continuous strip of paper that your health care professionals will be able to read. This monitor is attached to you by way of a simple belt worn around your belly.

If your pregnancy or labour is considered high risk, or if a problem arises during labour, the health team may need to use some form of constant internal monitoring to get a good idea of how the baby is doing, particularly during the contractions. This type of monitoring may be necessary if your baby is noted to have a heart rate that is too slow or too fast, or she has had a bowel movement, passing meconium (the first stool material) within the uterus.

Internal monitoring is done by attaching a scalp clip to a part of the baby that can be reached through the open cervix (usually the top of the head). This device reads and records the fetal heart rate (FHR). Sometimes it is necessary to take a sampling of blood from the baby's scalp so that her blood oxygen and pH levels can be checked (fetal scalp sampling).

When things are going slowly

Slow progress in labour is common. The appropriate rate varies, depending on how many babies you have had. With a first baby, for example, the time from the beginning of active labour to delivery will average 12 hours. You may be given an infusion of oxytocin (Syntocinon®), a synthetic hormone, to make your contractions more effective, particularly when dilation is occurring very slowly and your contractions are not frequent or strong enough. In several large studies, this "active management" of labour has been shown to decrease the rate of caesarean delivery. It also prevents labour from going on for an abnormally long time.

First stage of labour

The first stage of labour is divided into three parts: early, active, and transition. It is usually the longest part of the labour process.

Early in the pregnancy, your cervix is a thick-walled canal about 2.5 centimetres (one inch) long. During the last few weeks of your pregnancy, hormones will cause your cervix to soften. This is called the ripening of the cervix.

Once labour starts, contractions cause this ripened cervix to dilate, or open up, and to efface, or thin out. At the end of the first stage of labour, your cervix will be open 10 centimetres (four inches) and the sides will be very thin. At this point, your uterus, cervix, and vagina will be reshaped to form one long birth canal for the baby to pass through.

First stage—early—0-3 cm

In the very early part of the first stage of labour, you may wonder if you really are in labour. If you are not sure, come in to the hospital to the labour and delivery unit to get checked.

The chart on page 70 will help you to tell the difference between real and false labour. Your contractions will start about 15–20 minutes apart and last about 30–45 seconds. They will gradually occur closer together until they are less than five minutes apart. In the early stages, your cervix will soften and change. You may notice a thick bloody mucous discharge from your vagina, commonly called "show." At any point during labour, your water may break; that is, the membranes that contain the amniotic fluid may rupture.

Coping with early labour

You can:	Your labour coach can:
Tune into your body, go with the flow.	Have car ready and filled with gas.
At night, try to sleep.	Put your bags into the car.
During the day, alternate activity with rest.	Help you relax, offer you back or foot massages.
Take a warm bath or shower (unless your water has broken or is leaking).	If necessary, let people know labour has started.
Walk with your labour coach or watch a movie.	Encourage you to walk, rest, eat, and drink
Use relaxation techniques.	Time contractions from the beginning of one to the beginning of the next.
Breathe slowly and deeply through contractions.	Be calm and reassuring.
Keep your energy levels up by lightly eating and drinking.	Prepare you a light meal, offer you plenty of fluids.

First stage—active—3-8 cm

In the active part of the first stage of labour, you will notice the contractions are much stronger. They last about 45 seconds and occur about every 3–5 minutes. As the contractions progress, your cervix will continue to thin and open. At the end of this stage, your cervix should be eight centimetres open. You may begin to feel quite tired and anxious, making it very important to relax as much as you can between contractions. You may have back pain because of the position of the baby's head in your pelvis.

First stage—transition—8-10 cm

You are coming down the home stretch now. Your contractions may be every 2–3 minutes and will usually last about 60–90 seconds. This helps your cervix to dilate fully, to 10 centimetres. In many women, however, the labour actually slows down, and it may take longer to dilate the final two centimetres. At the same time that this is occurring, the baby's head should be slowly going down into the pelvis.

Coping with active labour

You can:

Relax, go with the flow of contractions.

Use light/quick breathing or a slow relaxation breathing.

Change positions often; don't lie on your back; moving will speed labour.

Expect contractions to get much stronger after water breaks.

Ask for pain relief if you want it.

Use visualization to help you to focus.

Take a warm bath to relax.

Use a birthing ball to put counter-pressure on your perineum and to help open up your pelvis.

Ask for help; make your needs known.

Empty your bladder as needed.

Your labour coach can:

Massage tense muscles.

Stay with you.

Help with your breathing, let your rhythm dictate the breathing pattern that is best for you.

Encourage and help you to change positions often. Use pillows for support. Walk with you. Help you to sit upright if you wish.

Apply firm counter-pressure to your back during contractions. Give back rubs between contractions.

Be your voice to the staff, let you focus on labour.

Encourage you, tell you how far you have come. Help you get through contractions one at a time and prepare for the next one.

Support your choices. Never criticize. Make the room as peaceful as possible. Be calm and reassuring.

Coping with the transition to second stage labour

You can:

Move around as much as you need to get comfortable.

If your cervix is not 10 centimetres dilated, and you have the urge to push, try pant-pant-blow breathing to avoid pushing.

Get through contractions one at a time. Try to think of the pains as closer together, not stronger.

Take a shower or tub bath if possible.

Envision your body opening up like a flower to let your baby move out.

Wash hands and face with a cool cloth. Change your gown.

Suck ice chips or sip water to keep your mouth moist.

Tell your labour coach or nurse if you have the urge to push.

Your labour coach can:

Support your choice of position.

Help with breathing. Maintain eye contact so that you feel connected to your labour coach and more in control.

Remind you labour's almost over; the baby's nearly out. Be calm, reassuring, and positive.

Rub tense muscles if you want, especially around the lower back where the baby's head may be applying pressure.

Help you with visualizations and relaxation.

Stroke your face, hair, or other part of your body if you like.

Offer ice chips, apply a cool cloth to your brow.

If you have the urge to push, help you to transition breathe (pant-pant-blow) to avoid pushing until the nurse comes.

Medication-free techniques to make labour easier

Labour tends to be easier if you are relaxed and confident, rather than tense and fearful. Many of the techniques that you and your support team use to make labour easier are geared toward helping you relax and remain in control of your body and your mind.

You and your labour coach will have learned and practised several different techniques in the weeks and months before labour began. What works for other women may not work for you.

Special breathing

Several special breathing techniques may help make your job easier and promote a sense of control over your body and mind. Sometimes you will follow your body's lead, and breathe in whatever manner feels right, but you may find some of the following techniques helpful.

1 *Slow breathing*

This slow, deep breathing technique has been known to work best in the early stage of labour by shifting your attention away from the contractions. Begin by taking a deep breath through your nose or mouth. Then, purse your lips and very slowly blow the air out. Usually the rate and rhythm of this comes naturally, but the rate should be like counting in for 3-4 counts, out 3-4 counts. Many labouring women do this type of slow breathing throughout their entire labour and it works well for them.

2 *Light/quick breathing*

This type of breathing has been known to work best during the active part of labour, when the contractions are coming more often and getting quite strong. When a contraction begins, start by breathing slowly in and out. As the contraction gets stronger, shorten your breaths. At the peak (strongest point) of the contraction, breathe lightly in and quickly out, making a puffing sound much like the panting of a dog. When the contraction starts to ease off, slow your breathing down again and then take a deep, cleansing breath.

3. Transition breathing (pant-pant-blow)

This type of breathing has been known to work best during the transition stage of labour when the labour is most intense and you may no longer be able to slow breathe. Transition breathing is commonly called pant-pant-blow breathing and can be quite useful in helping you avoid the urge to push against a cervix that is not fully dilated. It is done like this: take a deep breath in, then break your exhalation into two short pants, followed by a longer blow to empty your lungs.

Body positions

The position you put your body in can sometimes make labour easier. Many studies have been done to find out which positions are best for both you and your baby. You should feel free to labour in any position that helps to make your labour easier and to change positions as often as you want to. The use of pillows can be helpful to prop up your legs, arms, and belly. It is not a good idea to lie flat on your back during labour because the weight of the uterus may squeeze a large blood vessel against your spine, slowing the blood supply to the baby.

1. Sitting upright

When you sit up straight (or lean back just a bit), both you and your baby benefit. Studies show this position may help your uterus to contract and, therefore, may shorten the second stage of your labour. In addition, this sitting position seems to help the baby move down the birth canal. Further studies show that babies born to mothers who were sitting upright during the actual delivery had better oxygen levels in their blood. Mothers reported they liked this position because it was easier to see their baby, and to bond with the baby once it was born. Most hospitals have birthing beds that make this sitting position easier. This is the most common way of giving birth.

2. Lying on your side

You may lie on your side at one time or another during labour but you may not have thought of actually delivering your baby while lying on your side. This position for birth is sometimes required because some women feel more comfortable labouring on their side. From a medical point of view, this position is useful to help your doctor deliver your baby safely if you have certain heart conditions, hip joint problems, or varicose veins in your legs. Your labour coach will need to support your upper leg during the birth.

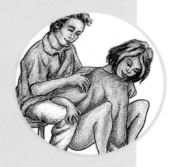

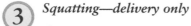 **Squatting—delivery only**

The squatting position has two benefits. First, the squatting position makes bearing down (pushing) easier because the uterus is able to fall forward with the force of gravity. This helps your baby to move down the birth canal. Second, studies show squatting helps to widen your pelvis, allowing more room for the baby to move down and out. North American women sometimes find this position uncomfortable because they are not used to it. Some hospitals provide birthing bars on their birthing beds to help women who choose to use this position.

④ **Kneeling on all fours—usually for delivery, or sometimes late in the first stage**

This position is a reasonable option for some women. Very few studies have been done about this position, but some experts believe it may help a baby turn around into the proper position for delivery if it hasn't done so on its own. Many women rock back and forth on all fours during contractions to help relieve their backache. This may be a useful position to try.

Hydrotherapy

Aside from giving comfort, there is good evidence that hydrotherapy (using showers, whirlpool baths, and tub baths) is beneficial to labouring women. Although hydrotherapy doesn't seem to shorten labour, it does seem to reduce a woman's stress. When a woman has less stress, more endorphins seem to be present in her body. Endorphins are the body's "feel good" hormone. In addition, less stress allows levels of the hormone oxytocin to rise in the body. This extra oxytocin helps the contractions to become more regular and stronger.

Before you begin water therapy, it is best to get help from your nurse. The water should not be too hot because the blood vessels that are close to the surface of your skin will dilate, which may cause your blood pressure to drop. This may make you feel dizzy.

If you spend a long time in the tub, it is important to drink fluids or to suck on ice-chips so that you don't become dehydrated. It is still important to empty your bladder as needed, but be very careful getting in and out of a slippery tub. During water therapy, your baby's heart rate will still need to be counted every now and then by your nurse. While in the tub, labouring mothers and their labour coaches can also do some of the other things that make labour easier, such as touch and massage therapy, visualization, and special breathing.

Hydrotherapy is usually limited to the first stage of labour.

Transcutaneous Electric Nerve Stimulation (TENS)

TENS is a safe, medication-free, non-invasive way to manage pain. It can help relieve pain by sending small electrical impulses through electrodes placed on the skin (on the belly or back) to the nerve fibres under the skin. TENS is believed to work in two different ways. First, the electrical impulses block a pain signal from being carried to the brain.

The contractions may be causing pain, but your brain doesn't sense it. TENS is also thought to work by triggering your body to release more endorphins—the body's "feel good" hormone.

If this method interests you, the physical therapy department of a hospital generally arranges TENS treatments. It may be beneficial to contact them before your labour, or to speak with your doctor about this method during a prenatal visit.

Vocalization

You may worry that you will cry out loudly during labour. Some women do and others don't. Nurses and doctors are very used to hearing and seeing labouring women use these methods to cope with the stress of labour. Many women vocalize during labour, others chant, moan, rock their bodies or heads from side to side, or cry. These are perfectly normal ways to cope with labour and you should never feel embarrassed if you feel the need to use these methods.

Using medication for pain relief

Two main types of medications are used to control pain during labour—painkillers or freezing. Painkillers are also known as analgesics. These medications dull the overall pain but do not cause a loss of feeling. Medications that "freeze" your body are called anesthetics. These medications cause a total loss of feeling in a certain area of the body. It is a good idea to talk about the kind of pain relief you would like in your birthing plan.

Painkillers (analgesics)

Most powerful painkillers are narcotics. Examples of narcotics you may be offered are meperidine (Demerol®) or morphine. Narcotics are usually given by an injection into the muscles of the hip, or sometimes through an intravenous (IV) line. They dull the pain and make you feel sleepy, so that you can rest between contractions, but they can cross through the placenta and may make your baby sleepy as well.

To ensure there is time for the effects of narcotics to wear off before the baby is born, narcotics are usually given in the early and active stages of your labour. In this way, your baby will be born alert and active. But if your baby is born sleepy because of a pain shot you needed, the doctors and nurses can safely give the baby an antidote called Narcan® that will quickly waken the baby.

Epidurals

An epidural block is a common procedure for giving an anesthetic medication to block the pain of labour and birth. In this procedure, a needle is inserted into a small space between the bones of your spine and the medication is injected into the space around the bundles of nerve endings found there. The medication numbs the nerves in that area and therefore blocks pain messages from going to your brain.

When the doctor puts the medication in place the first time, he will leave behind a small plastic tube (catheter) in the space between the bones, which will then be taped securely to the outside of your body. By doing this, your doctor is able to give you more of the medication if it is needed, without having to poke through your skin again with a needle.

Usually, the doctor will use this catheter to hook you up to a pump to enable the medication to be delivered a bit at a time. If you wish to use this type of pain control, it is best to discuss this with your doctor before you go into labour.

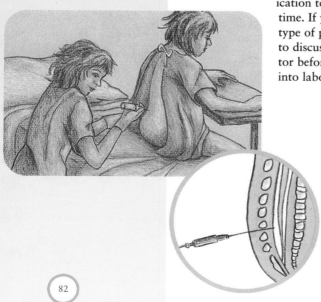

The second stage of labour

The cervix is now open 10 centimetres, or fully dilated. The baby is now ready to be pushed down the birth canal. During the second stage of labour, the contractions usually slow to 2–5 minutes apart and last about 45–90 seconds. This gives your body a well-needed rest period between contractions.

Pushing

Most women feel an urge to push when their baby reaches a certain point in their pelvis. Pushing offers some relief from the "pressure" of labour. Pushing through a contraction has been described as a powerful release of stored energy that comes from deep within a woman's body and mind. You may feel empowered, strengthened, and in control when you begin to push.

Some women, particularly if they have had an epidural, don't feel the urge to push and may need extra help and coaching to push their baby out.

When not to push

You may be asked to try not to push if your cervix is not quite ready (only 8–9 centimetres), or if your baby has not quite settled into the best position for pushing. However, sometimes the urge to push is so overpowering you are not able to resist it. With your nurse at your side to help you, you may be asked to put your knees very close to your chest and to use the pant-pant-blow method of special breathing until your cervix is completely open.

No urge to push

Some women go through a short period in which they don't have any contractions or their contractions are very light and they have no urge to push. This has been called the "rest and be thankful" period.

If your cervix is fully dilated but you don't feel an urge to push yet, relax and rest for a bit. The urge will come in time. Sometimes, epidurals can affect a woman's ability to push, or can inhibit the urge to push. Your nurse or doctor will give you support and advice.

The natural rhythm of pushing

There is no right or wrong way to push. Although it is still common to be encouraged to "take a deep breath in, hold it, and give one long steady hard push," studies show that this may not be the best method after all.

When women push naturally (without any instructions) they tend to do three to five short pushes during each contraction. As the second stage of labour moves along, the number of pushes per contraction tends to increase. With natural pushing, women take in several big breaths of air with each pushing effort, and slowly blow out all the air out of their lungs. Studies show that the natural way of pushing ensures the most oxygen reaches your baby during the second stage of labour. Sometimes this natural way

of pushing may take a few minutes longer. This can benefit you by allowing your skin more time to stretch (so the risks of tearing or the need for an episiotomy are less). A slow, controlled journey down the birth canal is easier on the baby.

Management of the delivery

In many cases, the delivery occurs without tearing. The birth attendant may attempt to massage the skin around the perineum, encouraging it to stretch. About 70 percent of first-time mothers will need some kind of small and simple repair to their perineum after childbirth. When the tears are repaired, the doctor may need to freeze the area with a local anesthetic to make it more comfortable. Research has shown that such small tears heal better, with less pain, than an episiotomy incision.

In some cases, it may be necessary to do an episiotomy if more room is needed to deliver the baby's head and shoulders, when there is a danger of severe tearing of the skin during childbirth, or if it is important to speed up the delivery because of concern for the baby.

An episiotomy is an incision about 2.5–5 centimetres (1–2 inches) long, made to the bottom of your vagina (perineum) toward the rectum or off to one side. Before the incision is made, the doctor will freeze the area with a local anesthetic.

Episiotomies should be done only if necessary, depending on the situation at the time of the birth.

Complete Breech

Frank Breech

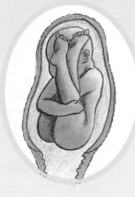

Footling Breech

84

Special delivery: complications in labour and delivery

Breech babies

Most babies lie with their heads down in the birth canal. The first part of the baby that can be felt in the birth canal is called the "presenting part." The presenting part in a normal delivery is the head. When a baby is breech, the head is up and the buttocks are down. In this case, the presenting part is the buttocks. This is called a frank breech. Sometimes one foot or both feet hang lower than the buttock and the foot (or feet) would be the presenting part. This is called a footling or incomplete breech.

When you reach full term and a breech baby is suspected, an ultrasound will be done to confirm the position, size, and health of your baby. A caesarean birth is best if: your baby appears to be larger than 4000 grams (8 1/2 pounds); or if the baby's head is tilted too far back (hyper-extended); or if the

umbilical cord is not in a good position; or if the amount of amniotic fluid is too low; or if it is a footling breech.

Otherwise, breech babies, particularly those in frank breech position, can safely be delivered vaginally. Breech babies are commonly monitored internally and externally. The choices for pain relief are the same as they are for a normal head-down delivery.

Assisted births: forceps or vacuum extraction

Sometimes a baby needs to be helped from the birth canal. A doctor may choose to assist the birth using forceps or a vacuum extraction.

The most common reason for an assisted birth is a prolonged second stage of labour, when the mother is fatigued and can no longer push, and the baby is low enough to be delivered vaginally with a little help. Another reason for an assisted birth is that, if a baby's heartbeat has slowed, the baby may be in trouble.

Both forceps and vacuum extractor methods are commonly used, safe, and very useful. Forceps are two slim, curved blades designed to slide around the baby's head inside the birth canal. Once they are in place, the doctor is able to gently pull the baby down and out with each contraction. There are several styles of forceps.

A better description of a vacuum-extraction-assisted birth might be a suction-assisted birth. In this case, a plastic cup, which is held in place by suction, is placed on top of the baby's head. A handle is attached to the cup, which enables the doctor to gently pull the baby down and out.

Breech vaginal deliveries are safe providing:

your baby is less than 4000 grams

the buttocks are showing first (frank or complete breech)

your pelvis is large enough for the baby to fit through

the level of amniotic fluid is normal

the cord is in a good position

the baby's head is well flexed

you are healthy.

Caesarean births

A caesarean section (also called a caesarean birth or a c-section) is the medical term for the surgical delivery of your baby from your uterus. In Canada, about 15 percent of women have caesarean births. Sometimes, for medical reasons, this surgery is scheduled and done before labour actually begins. Sometimes, if complications arise for the mother or the baby during labour, it is done when labour is already in progress.

The most common reason for a caesarean is "failure to progress in labour"—that is, despite good and regular contractions, the cervix stops dilating for several hours or the baby fails to descend into the pelvis for delivery. In these cases, and when other medical interventions have been tried without success (see page 84), a caesarean is necessary.

Concern about the baby's well-being is the second most common reason for a c-section. Usually, the concern is raised by changes in the baby's heart rate during labour, and is ideally confirmed with a fetal scalp blood sample. If either or both raise a strong suspicion that the baby may not be tolerating labour, and the birth is not imminent, a c-section will be considered.

The third most common reason for a caesarean is the mother's previous childbirths by c-section. It used to be said that "once a caesarean, always a caesarean." However, this is no longer true. In fact, about 60–80 percent of women who previously had a caesarean birth will be able to deliver vaginally.

If you have had a c-section before, it is important for you to know that you have an excellent chance of having a normal delivery. Studies have shown that many women do not want to try labour again because they are afraid of another long painful labour that will only end in another c-section. If this is how you feel, discuss this with your doctor. You need to be reassured that you will have adequate pain relief.

Other less common reasons for c-sections include particular types of breech presentation (page 84), or bleeding from a separated placenta or from a placenta located over the cervix. Sometimes a c-section is needed to preserve the health of the mother, as in the case of serious illness such as toxemia or severe cases of diabetes. If a mother has an active herpes infection, the baby will be delivered by c-section to prevent the disease from being transmitted to the baby during the birth.

Childbirth is an unpredictable experience that no one can fully control, no matter how prepared they may be. Whether you deliver your baby vaginally or by c-section, the goal of pregnancy is for you to become the mother of a healthy child. How you get to that goal is not as important as the goal itself. Although it is not always predictable, you should be aware that a c-section is a possibility. It may be a good idea to include a section in your birth plan that deals with what you would like to do if you need to have a caesarean birth.

Many healthy babies are delivered by caesarean birth to parents thankful this safe alternative for birthing exists. The need for an emergency caesarean birth is another good reason to deliver your baby in the safety of a hospital setting.

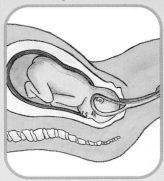

Forceps assistance

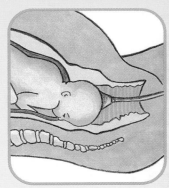

Suction assistance

The third stage of labour

This stage of labour begins after the baby has been born and ends when the placenta emerges. Other than having a few mild contractions to help push out your placenta, your work is done, and this is a time of relief.

As long as your uterus continues to shrink and stays firm (and if there is no unusual bleeding), it is best to take a watch-and-wait approach to the delivery of the placenta. Usually, the placenta will emerge within 30 minutes after the birth. Studies show it is helpful to clamp and cut the umbilical cord early after the birth to help shorten this time.

If you need any repairs to your skin from tearing or an episiotomy, they will be done once the placenta has been delivered. Finally, to help encourage your uterus to shrink, and therefore help to stop the bleeding, your doctor is likely to give you an injection of Syntocinon®, a synthetic hormone. Studies have shown that routine use of this hormone with the birth of the baby significantly reduces the amount of blood that a woman can lose after birth and can prevent postpartum hemorrhage.

During this time, your nurse will feel the size and shape of your uterus often to make sure it continues to shrink and the bleeding continues to slow down. Nurses will also be caring for your baby during this stage. You may tremble, feel chilled, or even a bit nauseated. The nausea should quickly pass and a warmed blanket will soothe your chills.

Cord blood gases

Immediately after birth, your doctor may do a "cord blood gases" test to determine if your baby needs extra help in adjusting to the outside world.

This test is done by taking a sample of blood from a section of the umbilical cord after it has been cut. The blood's oxygen level and the blood's pH level are checked. The pH level is used to measure the balance of chemicals in the blood, and is an important measure of the baby's well-being at birth.

The third stage of labour

You can:	Your labour coach can:
Relax. Hold and touch your baby.	Bond with the baby.
If you are shaky or chilled, ask for a warmed blanket.	Help you get set up to breastfeed.
Help push out the placenta when asked. (It is not painful.)	Offer you something to drink, wipe your face and hands with a damp cloth.

The fourth stage of labour

The fourth stage of labour begins after the placenta is out and lasts about two hours. It is a time to rest, enjoy, and recover. During this time, you will be watched very closely for any problems to arise. Your nurse will check your blood pressure, heart rate, breathing, the position of the top of your uterus, and the amount of bleeding from your vagina. It is during this stage, as both you and your baby adjust to the changes of childbirth, that you will have an important chance to bond with your baby.

Bonding with your baby

You probably began to care deeply for your baby before he was born. Fathers can bond just as deeply as mothers and should be given the chance to bond with their newborn within minutes after the birth. Some people feel love for their babies right away. For others, loving their baby takes time—rather like the difference between love at first sight and falling in love.

Unless there is a medical reason to do so, studies show it is best for you and your baby not to be separated after the birth. Consider keeping your baby unwrapped on your bare chest and abdomen, so that you have skin-to-skin contact during this time. This allows time for you to bond, to get to know each other. Bonding plays a very important role in helping you form a lifelong attachment to your baby.

Obstetrical nurses understand the bonding process and will encourage you. They will dim the lights, so the baby can open her eyes. Hold your baby closely, a few inches

from your face so the newborn can see you. Talk quietly and softly using your normal tone of voice. You may notice the baby's face turning toward the sound of your voice and her eyes searching to make contact with yours. Over the next few days, take advantage of every chance you get to talk to your baby. Hold her close and continue to get as much skin-to-skin contact as you can. Handle a newborn slowly and feed her whenever she seems hungry.

Apgar scores

A simple and quick method of testing newborns to see how fit and healthy they are is done one minute after the birth and again five minutes later. This test, called an Apgar Score, was developed by a paediatrician named Dr. Virginia Apgar. It is a very important and useful tool used to help doctors determine if your baby will need special care after the birth. There are five areas that are rated during an Apgar Score test: the baby's heart rate, breathing, muscle tone, reflexes, and skin colour. Depending on how the baby is responding, each area is rated and given a number ranging from zero to two (with zero being the poorest response and two being the best response). The total number is the Apgar Score. Most babies score between 7 and 10.

	score 0	score 1	score 2
Heart rate	Absent	Slow (<100 per minute)	100 per minute
Breathing	Absent	Weak	Good, strong cry
Muscle tone	Limp	Some movements	Active movements
Reflexes	No response	Grimace, whimpering	Cough or sneeze
Skin colour	Blue or pale	Body pink, arms and legs blue	Completely pink

A baby who was born with a heart rate of 140 (scores 2), and a good strong cry (scores 2), with some movements (scores 1), coughing (scores 2) and pink all over (scores 2) will have an Apgar score of 9. Any score over 7 at 5 minutes predicts a healthy baby.

People to call after the baby arrives

_____

_____

_____

_____

_____

_____

_____

_____

_____

_____

_____

_____

For the first hour or two after the birth, both mother and baby are very alert, so this is an optimum time for both bonding and the first breastfeeding.

Allow your baby to rest peacefully and give her time to adapt to the new surroundings. Within a few days, you two will know each other better. Within a few weeks, your new baby will know the world is a good and safe place to be.

Postpartum hemorrhage

Bleeding too much after the birth (postpartum hemorrhage) happens to about 7–10 out of every 100 women. It can be quite worrisome. For the most part, uncontrolled bleeding happens for two reasons: a uterus that will not contract, or retained placenta fragments. Postpartum hemorrhage can quickly become life threatening and is one of the main reasons why it is best to deliver your baby in a hospital.

In the past, women died of this complication, but with modern medical care, postpartum hemorrhage is usually easy to stop. Postpartum hemorrhage is more common if the baby was large or the labour long and difficult, or if there were multiple births (twins).

When the placenta separates from the inside wall of the uterus, blood vessels are left open-ended and leaking. The body's way of closing these blood vessels is to make the uterus clamp down tightly to squeeze them closed. The most common reason for uncontrolled bleeding after birth is a soft uterus that doesn't clamp down fast enough or hard enough to close off these open blood vessels to seal them off. If this is the cause of the bleeding, the uterus must be stimulated (with medication) to contract in order to stop the bleeding.

The placenta should come out in one piece. If it breaks apart and pieces of the placenta stay inside the uterus, the pieces are "retained." This is the second most likely cause for bleeding after birth. When this happens, even the normal clamping and sealing off of the blood vessels by the uterus is not enough to stop the bleeding. If the placenta cannot be completely removed, you may need an operation (a D&C) right away to remove the retained pieces of placenta from the inside of the uterus.

Preventing postpartum hemorrhage

It is best to try to prevent postpartum hemorrhage before it starts. Recent studies show that giving women hormone-like medications (oxytocin) can prevent the risk of postpartum hemorrhage by up to 40 percent. Because of this benefit, most hospitals now give these medications routinely, either during the second or third stage of labour. The medications are given by injection into a muscle, or into your vein.

Breastfeeding and massaging a soft uterus are two other valuable ways to prevent postpartum bleeding because both stimulate the uterus to contract.

How long will you stay in hospital?

Benefits of going home early

The length of time a new mother and her baby stay in the hospital after the birth has become much shorter over recent years. Although some of this change has been related to reduction in spending on health care, going home early can be better for both of you. Providing your baby is healthy and that you will have plenty of support at home, and if your hospital offers a follow-up home care program, you will probably be discharged 24–48 hours after the birth. Studies show that by going home soon after the birth of your healthy baby, you are more likely to adjust better to being a new mom. Your home is quieter and more relaxed than the hospital and you will probably sleep better in your own bed. Efforts to breastfeed may be more successful in the familiar comfort of your own home and your baby is less likely to get an infection. Most importantly, it is easier for the baby's father and the rest of the family to spend time with the newest member of the family at home.

The maternity nurses are experts in teaching new mothers ways to care for their newborn babies. It is always a good idea to learn what you can from them during your hospital stay. Don't be shy about asking all the questions you have about anything, even if you think the question may be unimportant.

Follow-up home care

In most communities, a public health nurse does follow-up home care within two days. If you are going home early, it is very important that there be early follow-up of the baby, preferably with a home visit from a nurse.

The Society of Obstetricians and Gynaecologists of Canada and the Canadian Paediatric Society have issued a combined statement of the ways to know when it is safe for mothers and babies to leave hospital early. They recommend early home follow-up as essential to early discharge.

The most important reason for this is to make sure feeding is well established and the baby is getting adequate fluid and nutrition in her first days.

During a home visit, the nurse will examine you and your baby and will answer all your questions about caring for yourself and your newborn. This visit usually includes discussions about your body, breastfeeding, diapering, bathing, bonding with your baby, having sex again, birth control, and any other topic you feel a need to ask questions about. This private and close care is proving to be a very good way to give new mothers the confidence they need to look after their new babies. It is a good idea to write your questions down before the nurse arrives, so that you will remember what you wanted to ask.

Longer hospital stays

Sometimes, it is best to stay in the hospital a little longer than usual. This may happen if there were problems during the birth, if you had a long labour, or if you or your baby need special care or rest. In addition, a longer hospital stay may be important if your hospital does not offer a community-based home care program or if you do not have enough support at home. Talk to your obstetrical nurse or your doctor if you have concerns about going home.

Follow-up home care information

Public health clinic phone number:

_____

First visit date and time:

_____

Second visit date and time:

_____

Public health nurse's name:

_____

Things I need to ask the public health nurse during my home visit:

1. _____

2. _____

3. _____

4. _____

5. _____

If things don't go well for your baby

Most babies are born perfect in every way but, despite advances in modern medicine, babies are sometimes born seriously ill or with birth defects. Very rarely, babies die. All parents hope for the best during pregnancy and most have bonded deeply with their unborn child before the birth. They begin to think of their baby as a person, as the newest member of their family.

It is a great shock when a baby is born with birth defects or without signs of life. Many mothers feel their bodies have betrayed them, that their bodies have let everyone down, including the baby and her partner. Some worry they did something to cause the birth defect or loss of life. This is almost never true.

Parents can feel a deep sense of loss even if the baby is born alive but is born with serious birth defects or an illness. They grieve for the child with whom they cannot share a normal life.

The deepest and most profound sense of loss comes with the death of a baby. Many parents, understandably, have trouble coping with their loss. Such a sudden tragedy causes intense sadness, shock, disbelief, and anger.

For parents and family, the grieving process is a necessary part of healing. Grieving helps parents cope. All parents need bereavement support at such a tragic time in their lives.

Say goodbye to your baby

You can help create memories of your baby by giving yourself a chance to hold your baby and say goodbye. If your baby died because of birth defects, you may be afraid to see him, but in almost all cases, what the parents imagine is worse than it really is.

You may want to have a memorial service or funeral or you may choose a private ceremony. As grieving parents, you need to be able to talk about your feelings. Your baby is a real part of your life.

Nurses have done studies that show that parents need bereavement support to help them to deal with their grief, so many hospitals have a process available to grieving parents.

You and your partner

Your relationship with your partner may suffer from the loss. You may find you have trouble talking to one another and cannot face each other. You may find it hard to do the normal things you used to do. It may be hard to start making love again. You may have unresolved feelings of anger at the other person and not know why. You may be searching for someone to blame. It is normal to feel this way.

Be patient with each other. Tell each other how you are feeling and be as open and honest as you can. Seek professional counselling. If your partner can't talk about the baby's death right now, remind yourself that you will be able to talk to each other about it in the future. Your baby is not forgotten. Everyone grieves in their own way and at their own pace.

Make an extra effort to be tender toward your partner. Be reassuring to each other, use touch to show you care. Your baby was conceived out of your love for each other. Hold tight to the memories of your lives together before tragedy struck and know that some day peace will find you again.

Touch her Todays

Your loving touch has the power to soothe your baby and lull her to sleep. Touch calms her and comforts her, and may play a role in healing. To your baby, touch is love, the first way she learns to love and trust in return.

Johnson & Johnson

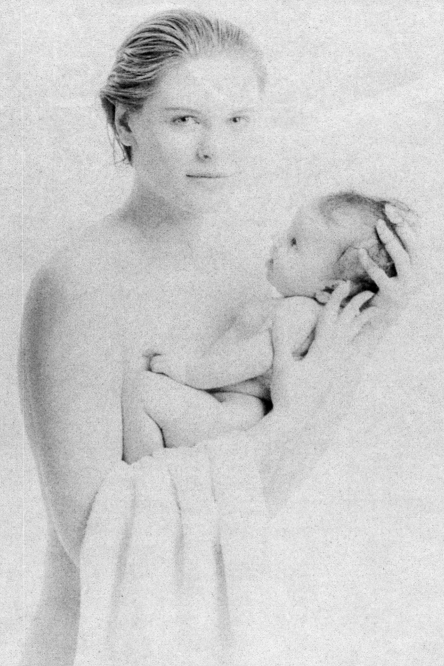

Ask your doctor about progestin only pills

JAMI98

Chapter Seven

Taking care of yourself

Recipe for rest

Many new mothers have a burst of energy right after the baby is born and then feel very tired. Your baby will be hungry every 2–3 hours or so for the first little while, and it may seem as though the feeding cycle never really ends. This is perfectly normal but it does take a great deal of energy to keep up such a busy schedule. It is very important to get enough rest. Sleep when the baby sleeps. We'll say that again... It is very important to get enough rest. Here is an easy recipe to remember:

O ne of the most important things you can do for your new baby is to take care of yourself. It is easier to look after a newborn if you are rested and healthy. You will need time to get used to all the changes having a baby brings. Your body has gone through many changes during pregnancy, and now you are not pregnant any more. That alone is a lot to get used to. Getting back to the way you used to be before you were pregnant takes time. This is a good time to ask for the help of family and friends or to accept their offers to help cook meals, clean house, do laundry, or babysit other children.

(R) Relax whenever you can. Take a nap, read, watch television and again, sleep when the baby sleeps!

(E) Eat well and drink plenty of fluids, especially if you are breastfeeding.

(S) Share the responsibility of your new baby with your partner, family, and friends. Ask for help.

(T) Take the time to enjoy the baby. Cuddle, coo, sing to your baby. Let the housework wait.

Your changing body (postpartum)

The many changes your body went through during pregnancy took place over more than nine months. Realistically, it will take about the same amount of time for things to return to normal, so be patient with yourself. After delivery, your uterus is round and hard. It is about 17.5 centimetres long (seven inches). You can feel the top of it at about the level of your navel. Six weeks after the birth, your uterus will be about 7.5 centimetres (three inches) long. You won't be able to feel it any more by pressing on your abdomen. Breastfeeding helps the uterus to shrink back to its normal size more quickly.

The area between your rectum and your vagina is called your perineum. It will have stretched during the delivery. Your perineum may feel swollen, bruised, and tender. You may have stitches from a tear or episiotomy. The stitches will dissolve over time. While they heal, they can be itchy. Continue with your Kegel exercises (page 34) after six weeks. They will help the stretched muscles in your perineum regain their tone. Some women experience a sensation of numbness in their perineum, which passes over time.

The baby blues

After giving birth, it is normal to cry for no reason, to feel anxious, frightened, and sad. More than 70 percent of all new mothers feel a little depressed after the baby is born. This mild depression is thought to be linked to the changing levels of pregnancy hormones. It may also be linked to feelings of loss, since the baby is no longer inside you. Usually the baby blues start within a couple of days of the birth. They may last for hours or days. Normally, they go away within two weeks without any treatment.

You may feel a wide range of changing emotions. One minute you feel happy and the next minute you feel sad. You may feel very tired, then get a burst of energy. You may have trouble sleeping or making decisions. You may feel confident, then insecure. You may feel as though you will never get your life back or your body back into shape. You may feel tired all the time and may not be interested in sex at all. All of these feelings are completely normal. Now is the perfect time to reach out to your partner, family, and friends for love, support, and help.

When "the blues" turn into depression

If the baby blues seem to be getting worse instead of better, or if they last more than two weeks, you may be developing postpartum depression. This happens to a small number of new mothers. Your feelings of sadness have turned to deep despair and a sense of hopelessness. You may resent being on call 24 hours a day, every day. You may love all the attention the baby gets and feel jealous at the same time. You may feel in charge and then angry that you are in charge. You may begin to question your ability to look after your baby. You may feel very frustrated and even angry when the baby cries, and may think the baby is crying just to annoy you. You may think about harming the baby or yourself and may even tell yourself these feelings you are having are not normal. Treatment is available for postpartum depression. Get help right away. Talk to your public health nurse or your doctor about your feelings.

Recognizing signs of postpartum depression

If any of these apply to you, get help:

- ○ My baby blues haven't gone away after two weeks.
- ○ I have strong feelings of sadness or guilt.
- ○ I have strong feelings of hopelessness or helplessness.
- ○ I can't sleep, even when tired.
- ○ I sleep all the time, even when my baby is awake.
- ○ I am not able to eat, even when hungry.
- ○ I am not able to eat because I am never hungry or because I feel sick.
- ○ I worry about the baby too much; I'm obsessed about him.
- ○ I don't worry about the baby at all; it's almost like I don't care.
- ○ I am having panic attacks.
- ○ I have feelings of anger toward the baby.
- ○ I think about harming myself or my baby.

If you have any of these signs, get help right away. If you know a new mother who has these signs of depression, get help for her. Counselling and treatment will help the feelings go away. Don't wait, call your doctor.

Signs of bleeding problems

It is not normal for your flow to stay heavy or become heavier. Normally, you would notice that your flow is gradually decreasing with each passing day. If your flow has been slowing down and suddenly you develop a lot of heavy, bright red blood (which soaks through one or more maxi-pads within two hours and does not slow or stop with rest) do not wait, go to the hospital immediately. This most commonly happens around the third or fourth week after giving birth, but can happen sooner or later.

In addition, it is not normal for you to develop large blood clots. It is also abnormal to notice an unusual discharge or foul smell coming from your vagina. If this happens, it may mean you have developed an infection at the site of your episiotomy or a vaginal infection. This can be serious and you should call your doctor right away. You may need antibiotics. If your flow has not completely stopped after five weeks, make an appointment to see your doctor.

Normal vaginal discharge

The vaginal discharge after birth is called *lochia*. It is made up of blood and tissue from the lining of the uterus. The lochia is bright red at first. It may contain a few small clots. Bright red blood may flow again for short periods during or after breastfeeding. This is normal and due to the mild contractions of the uterus breastfeeding causes. If blood has had a chance to collect in the vagina while you are lying down, it can gush out for a short time when you stand up. This is also normal for the first few days. Within a few days, your flow will become lighter and pinker. It is also normal to notice blood spotting occasionally during the time your flow is decreasing. Eventually your flow will turn whitish or yellow and gradually stop. The overall length of time a woman flows can vary from 10 days to five weeks. If you are a second-time mother, your flow may not be the same as it was with your last baby.

If the flow is heavier than you think is normal, is heavier than a period, or the smell is foul, check with your doctor. It is best to use pads, not tampons.

Menstrual periods

If you are not breastfeeding, your menstrual period will start again 4–9 weeks after the birth. Your period may be longer, shorter, heavier, or lighter than before pregnancy. It should return to what is normal for you after a few cycles. If you are breastfeeding, menstruation may not start again for months or not until you stop breastfeeding altogether. But, your ovaries may begin to work before your period returns. This means you could become pregnant again without ever having your period. If you wish to avoid pregnancy, you should begin using birth control as soon as you plan to resume sexual relations (usually 4–8 weeks) after the birth.

Having sex again

When to have sex again is a personal choice. It is safe to do so once the bleeding has stopped but you should have sex again only when you feel ready. You should not let yourself feel rushed into having sex. Your body, mind, and spirit need time to adjust to the changes childbirth and motherhood bring. If you are like most new mothers, you will probably use all the energy you have to look after the baby. You may feel quite tired for the first few weeks.

You may worry that sexual intercourse may be painful. If it is, special jellies or creams are helpful to lubricate the vagina. You could try changing positions to see if one is more comfortable than another. You may feel mildly depressed and not be interested in sex. Some new mothers feel insecure about their changed body image and may not feel attractive for the first little while. All of these feelings and worries are completely normal.

Some men don't feel like having sex too soon after the baby is born, either. They too may feel a bit worn out by late-night feedings, all the excitement, and their added sense of responsibility. Most men recognize that you need the time to recover from the birth, both emotionally and physically.

Most couples don't have sex for weeks, some don't have sex for months. This does not mean your relationship is in trouble. It only means that you are both taking time to adjust to the changes a baby brings. It is very important to trust each other and talk about your feelings. There are many non-sexual ways to show your partner how you feel. If you have any concerns about resuming sexual relations with your partner, make an appointment with your doctor for a checkup. For a discussion of birth control choices, see pages 97-98.

Common discomforts after giving birth

Tender breasts

When your milk comes in, about 2–4 days after the baby is born, your breasts may become very full, sore, and hard (see page 108 for a discussion of engorgement). If you are breastfeeding, feed your baby often to help drain the milk glands. Pump the milk from your breasts to relieve the pressure. Warmed towels applied to your breasts may be soothing.

If you are not breastfeeding, ice packs may help reduce the swelling, but do not empty or pump your breast as this will only cause more milk to be produced. If you are not breastfeeding, take pain medication. When your breasts are tender, good support is important and it helps to wear a well-fitting support bra, even at night.

Vaginal pain

It is normal for the perineum, the area around your anus and vagina, to be swollen, bruised, and tender after you have given birth. For some women, this soreness lasts up to six weeks. If you have stitches, you may feel even more discomfort. Try this: dampen and freeze a clean maxi-pad. Put the frozen pad in your underwear. This should help reduce swelling. Sometimes a warm bath helps relieve the itching caused by healing stitches. Keep the vaginal area clean to avoid infection. Get plenty of rest with your feet up to take the pressure off your bottom. If you need it, take pain medication.

Cramping

Pains that feel like strong menstrual cramps are called afterpains. They are caused by the uterus as it shrinks. Afterpains may be worse during breastfeeding. First-time mothers may not feel afterpains. Try taking a warm bath, or put a heating pad across your abdomen. Pain medication sometimes helps, particularly those medications meant for menstrual cramps. The deep breathing and relaxation techniques you learned during pregnancy may also help.

Bowel movements

It is perfectly normal if you do not have a bowel movement for 2–3 days after the birth of your baby. Your bowel is sluggish if you haven't eaten much or if you received painkillers. In addition, the abdominal muscles you need to help push out a bowel movement are stretched and not as effective.

Many women fear the first bowel movement will be painful because of hemorrhoids or a bruised perineum. They may "hold back" having a bowel movement for this reason. Try not to do this. Holding back may make your stool hard. Instead, do what you can to avoid hard stools. Drink plenty of fluids and fruit juice and eat foods high in fibre, such as bran muffins, bran cereal, fresh fruit, and vegetables. Stool softeners are available at the drugstore. Hard, difficult stools may cause hemorrhoids. Mild exercise, such as walking (inside the house or outside), often helps to get the bowel moving and will help eliminate painful gas.

Hemorrhoids

Grape-like lumps around the rectal opening are hemorrhoids. They are often painful and itchy. During a difficult bowel movement, they may ooze bright red blood. To help bring down the swelling, try freezing a dampened maxi-pad and putting the frozen pad in your underwear. Choose to lie down, rather than sit, to take the pressure off your bottom until the hemorrhoids heal. Some of the special creams, sprays, and ointments sold to help shrink the swelling of hemorrhoids are effective. Talk to your pharmacist and doctor.

Urination

Immediately after the birth or for the first day or so, you may find it hard to urinate if you had a catheter, or painful if you have stitches in place or a small tear in your vagina. To help the flow of urine get started, try turning on the taps in the bathroom sink so you can hear the water. To help take away the sting, try urinating while taking a shower or bath or squeezing warm water from a bottle over the area when you void. Avoid rubbing the toilet paper over the area after urinating. Instead, hold a wad of toilet paper in place and let it soak up the urine like a sponge.

Later, you may find you have to urinate quite often or that you have trouble knowing when the urine is going to start to flow. You may lose urine with a cough, sneeze, or physical activity. This problem is called urinary incontinence. It is caused by the stretching of the pelvic floor muscles. You can help strengthen your muscles by doing Kegel exercises (page 34). For most women, this problem gradually goes away. In the meantime, special absorbent underwear and pads have been designed to protect your clothing and avoid embarrassing situations. Talk to your pharmacist.

The shape you're in

If your abdomen is flabby and you think you still look pregnant after the birth, you are perfectly normal. Try not to worry about it. Your abdominal muscles stretched a great deal during your pregnancy and they don't just spring back into place once the baby is born. It takes time for them to slowly tighten back into their pre-pregnant shape. The weight you gained happened gradually, and it may take a few months to lose it. Don't try to lose weight quickly by following a low-calorie diet. It is far better to eat a variety of healthy foods and resume exercise activity as soon as you can.

Invest in as good a stroller or carriage as you can afford—second-hand is fine, or you may be able to borrow. Look for one that is easy to walk with. Walking at a good pace is excellent toning exercise, and your little one will enjoy it too. The latest weight-loss research has shown that as little as 20 minutes a day of brisk walking or similar exercise will affect your metabolism, so that you "burn" more calories. Severely restricting your diet will have the opposite effect, as your body adjusts to "famine conditions" by storing as much energy as possible as fat.

In some communities, you may be able to find postnatal fitness classes specifically geared to the fat-burning and toning exercises needed by new mothers. These classes have another benefit—you will meet other new mothers and talk about the things that are on your mind. If you are short of sleep and finding meeting all of your baby's needs stressful, this informal sharing can help.

Breastfeeding your baby will help you lose weight because your body needs to burn extra calories in order to produce the energy it takes to make breast milk. In addition, breastfeeding stimulates the uterus to contract and shrink back to its normal size.

Birth control choices

If you do not want to get pregnant, you and your partner should decide what type of birth control is best for you now. You can get pregnant while you are breastfeeding, and you can get pregnant even if your periods haven't started yet. When you and your partner begin having sex again, be prepared by already having everything you need close by. Talk to your doctor.

Birth control pills are a good choice for most women. They are best started 3-4 weeks after delivery. If you are breastfeeding, the hormones in the pill have not been found to affect the baby. However, they can affect your milk supply. You should be fine if your breastfeeding is well established and you are producing plenty of milk. But if your milk supply has been low, ask your doctor about using a progestin-only type of pill, as these appear not to affect milk production.

When you do start taking the pill, follow the instructions carefully. You are not safe until you have completed one full cycle of pills. In the meantime, use other methods.

Latex condoms for men are easy to use and help protect both partners against sexually transmitted disease. They are a good choice to have on hand, just in case. Follow the directions carefully.

Female condoms are now available at your local drugstore. Be sure to purchase the latex type and follow the instructions carefully.

Spermicidal foams and creams kill sperm. These are most reliable when used with a latex condom. Follow the directions carefully.

Diaphragms cover the opening to the uterus to prevent sperm from entering. If you used a diaphragm before you were pregnant, you will need to have a new one fitted, but not until eight weeks after the birth. Diaphragms are most reliable when used in combination with spermicidal foams or creams.

Depo-Provera® is the name of the drug used to prevent pregnancy. It is given by injection, once every three months. It is safe, easy, and economical. Talk to your doctor.

An intra-uterine device (IUD) is a good choice for some women, and can be fitted in the doctor's office eight weeks after the birth, when your uterus has returned to its normal size. Talk to your doctor.

For more information, look in your phone book under Planned Parenthood, birth control, family counselling, or public health clinics.

If you have completed your family

Sterilization is permanent birth control. Although there is a possibility that sterilization procedures can be reversed surgically, you and your partner should consider your decision carefully.

Vasectomy is a sterilization procedure for men. It is performed using local anesthetic in the office of a urologist, a medical specialist. The *vas deferens*, which is the tube that carries sperm from the testicles, is cut.

Tubal ligation is a form of sterilization for women. It is performed in hospital, under a general anesthetic. A number of surgical options are available.

Your follow-up visit

Recording your progress after birth or postpartum

Date:

Blood pressure:

Weight:

We think everyone should always travel in comfort and safety.

1-888-TOYOTA-8 · www.toyota.c

Chapter Eight

Taking care of your baby

Signs of dehydration in newborns

Dehydration can be very serious. Your baby may be dehydrated if you notice any of the following signs.

Call your doctor immediately.

sunken eyes
sunken soft spot on the top of the baby's head
drowsy, sleepy, hard to wake up
restless and irritable
breathing faster than 40 times a minute
less urine (wets less often, or diapers not as wet)
dark yellow urine
dry mouth, lips, tongue, nose
weight loss
firm belly
fever

Newborn babies have special needs. They need to be handled slowly, gently, and firmly. They cannot control their muscles or hold up their heads. When you pick them up you will need to support the two heaviest parts of their bodies—their heads and their bottoms. Newborn babies may have a coating of waxy vernix covering their body. When this is washed off, their skin may peel from the dryness. Many newborns have fine hair along their backs and shoulders. This usually disappears in a week or two. They may have white spots, rashes, or blotchy skin patches that usually clear up in a few days. Some newborns have bluish-grey skin around their fingers and toes. This is caused by changes in their circulation after birth and usually goes away in a few days.

The head may have been molded into an odd shape during the baby's journey down the birth canal. Over the next few weeks or months, the baby's head will become a normal shape. On top of the baby's head you will feel two soft spots, called fontanelles, where the bones have not grown together yet. If you watch closely, you will see them pulse up and down. This is normal. Touching the fontanelles will not harm the baby. The bones in the skull usually grow together by the time a baby reaches 18 months of age. Some newborns have a full head of hair while others have none. Some babies lose their hair only to have it grow back a different colour. The colour of the baby's eyes may change over the next three to six months.

The hormones in your body at the time of the birth may cause changes in your baby's body. For example, newborns of both sexes may develop swollen breasts when they are a few days old and some babies' breasts leak a few drops of milk. Don't worry about this milk. It will go away by itself. Pregnancy hormones may cause the baby's sex organs to be larger than normal for a few days. A baby boy may have a reddened scrotum (sac that holds his testicles). Baby girls may have a bit of bleeding or white discharge from their vaginas. All of these are normal.

Your baby's elimination

It is vitally important that your baby's elimination system is working properly. You can tell if all is well by the number of times your baby soils or wets his diaper. Newborns can become dehydrated very quickly. Dehydration can lead to serious problems for babies. Therefore, giving your baby plenty of milk and watching to be sure your baby has normal amounts of feces and urine are very important.

A baby's first bowel movement is called meconium. It is a tarry and greenish-black-substance. Babies will pass meconium for about 24–48 hours after birth. After that, the stool will become looser and greenish-yellow, called transitional stool, for 3-4 days. A breastfed baby's stool is golden yellow (like mustard), sometimes loose—even watery—sometimes seedy, mushy, curdly, or the consistency of mustard.

Breastfed babies may soil their diapers many times during a 24-hour period and are rarely constipated. However, some breastfed babies have bowel movements only every few days. Formula-fed babies' feces are more solid, yellow to green in colour, and have a strong odour. Formula-fed babies tend to have more problems with constipation.

You will know your baby is getting enough milk if the urine is almost clear and hard to see in the diaper but you can still feel the diaper is wet or heavier than a dry diaper. Very yellow urine may mean your baby is dehydrated and needs more milk (fluids). Make sure you check the diaper every time you change your baby to make sure it is wet. If there is plenty of fluid going in, then plenty of fluid (urine) should come out.

Newborns who lose more than five percent of their total body fluids can become seriously ill. Read the signs of dehydration in newborns. Call your doctor if you have any concerns.

Diapering your baby

Since newborns wet up to 18 times a day, and move their bowels as often as 10 times a day, you will need to have plenty of clean diapers on hand. To keep your baby's skin clean and dry, change your baby each time the diaper is dirty. Most parents tend to establish a diaper-changing routine. For example, some parents change the baby after each feeding, before laying the baby down for a nap. Others find that changing their baby's diaper is an effective way to wake a sleepy baby that still needs to nurse from the other breast.

There are two kinds of diapers: cloth or disposable. Cloth diapers are a better choice if you are concerned about contributing to environmental waste or about the cost of disposables. Many communities have diaper services that will pick up soiled and wet diapers and deliver freshly laundered ones. If you have a washer and dryer at home, you may find washing your own is not too difficult or time consuming.

Cord care

The stump of the umbilical cord usually shrivels up and falls off in a week or two. The spot underneath will be the baby's belly button. It is important to keep this stump

Safety tips for changing diapers

 Get everything you need before you lay the baby down to be changed.

You will need:

- small washcloths or disposable baby wipes
- clean diaper and maybe clean clothes
- rubbing alcohol and Q-tips until the cord comes off
- ointment to prevent diaper rash

 Never turn your back on your baby, not even for a second!

 Put your hand on the baby's tummy if you must reach for something. If you can't reach, take the baby with you.

 Ignore a ringing doorbell or phone, or take the baby with you to answer them.

 Wash your hands after each time you change your baby, to prevent the spread of germs.

About jaundice

When some babies are a few days old, their skin and the whites of their eyes may turn a yellowish colour. This is called jaundice. Jaundice is caused by the build-up of a green substance in the baby's blood called bilirubin. Bilirubin is formed when the baby's body breaks down old red blood cells. It is the liver's job to remove bilirubin but a newborn's liver doesn't start removing bilirubin until the baby is a few days old. During pregnancy, the mother's liver and the placenta removed the bilirubin.

If your baby becomes jaundiced you should not worry. The levels that most babies develop don't usually cause problems. High levels of bilirubin in the blood can harm a baby's nervous system, but this is rare. A baby's blood can be tested by the nurse during her home visit or by your doctor. Rarely, your baby will be treated in the hospital using phototherapy. Phototherapy is done by placing a baby under special lights.

clean and to prevent infection. Ask your doctor, maternity nurse, or public health nurse which solution, if any, is best applied to the stump. Cleaning the cord does not hurt the baby but some solutions feel cold and may cause the baby to cry. Don't use gauze or bandages on the stump. The cord area should be cleaned at least three times a day.

To keep the cord clean, fold the top of the diaper away from the stump. This also helps to keep it dry. The cord may be infected if the area around the cord becomes red, swollen, smells bad, or has pus coming out. Call your doctor if you think your baby's cord is infected. After the cord falls off, continue cleaning the belly button for a few more days.

If you think your baby has jaundice:

Feed the baby every 2–3 hours during the day and night.

Call your doctor.

Your doctor will want to know:

• the number of soiled and wet diapers your baby has had

• the quantity and colour of the stools in soiled diapers

Instructions from your doctor or health nurse:

_____

_____

_____

Eye care

After the baby was born, the nurse placed special drops (or an ointment) in the baby's eyes to prevent infection from germs that could enter the eye during the birth. Unless signs of infection appear, such as redness or a discharge from the eye, all you need to do is wipe each closed eye with a moist cloth to keep the area clean. If you think the baby's eyes are infected, call your doctor or the public health nurse.

Dressing

Babies need the same layers of clothing as their parents are wearing. In the winter, they may need an undershirt, a shirt, and a sweater along with warm coverings on their legs, socks or booties, and a snowsuit. In the summer, they may be most comfortable in only a T-shirt and diaper. In air-conditioned rooms or cars, your baby may need more clothes than you do because he is not active. Babies tend to feel cold sooner than you would.

Bathing

It is important to keep your baby clean, but until baby starts getting down and dirty on all fours, a daily bath is not necessary. Sponge baths are a good choice for the first few days until the cord has healed. You may use mild baby soaps to clean the skin. Use a moisturizing cream like Glaxal® Base to soothe dry skin. Pay special attention to the scalp and the folds in the baby's skin. After a few days, once her own body temperature has had a chance to adjust to life outside the uterus, it is all right to give a full bath even if the cord has not yet fallen off. For safety reasons, it is best to use a baby bathtub, not your regular tub. Gather everything you need first. Fill the basin with about two inches of warm water. Test the water using the inside of your wrist to make sure it is not too hot, and **never leave a baby alone in a tub, even for one second.**

Feeding your baby

The time you spend feeding your baby is a special time for both of you. Babies thrive on feeling your warmth and love as you hold them. They also love to suck and love the feeling of being full of warm milk. Many new mothers feel a close bond forming with their babies when they feed them. To a newborn, feeding time is heavenly.

The Society of Obstetricians and Gynaecologists of Canada and the Canadian Paediatric Society recommend breast milk as the best food for babies for a minimum of six months, but preferably longer. No commercial formula is exactly like breast milk, although some formulas come close.

When to call the doctor

Call your doctor right away if your baby:

- has a temperature of more than 38.5°C (100° F)

- has a seizure (shaking body, arms, and legs)

- has trouble breathing (works hard to suck air in, lips and ear lobes blue/grey coloured)

- has pale skin that feels cold and moist

- vomits more than twice in one day (large amounts of vomit, not the spit-up kind)

- has diarrhea more than twice in one day (large watery stools)

- passes blood or blood clots

- wets fewer than six diapers a day

- nurses poorly or refuses to eat

- seems weak, can barely cry

- cries more than usual, cries differently, acts very fussy, and nothing you seem to do works to make the baby stop crying

- doesn't act like he or she used to, seems "different" somehow, wakes up less alert, sleeps more than the usual amount

When an otherwise healthy baby gets sick, it can happen quickly. If you are concerned about your baby for any reason, call your doctor.

Breastfeeding tips

- Ask the nurses to make sure your baby is latching on properly before you go home.

- Be sure to drink water often during the day.

- Get comfortable before you begin nursing. Gather everything you need so you don't have to keep getting up.

- Burp your baby before you start.

- Start with one breast, letting the baby nurse for as long as he likes.

- The baby will fall asleep, stop sucking or let go of your breast when finished.

- Take a break. Burp your baby. Change a soiled diaper and wash your hands. (This often stimulates the baby to wake up and continue feeding. Nursing is tiring work for a newborn.)

- Start again with the other breast. If the baby won't take any more, try to remember to start with this breast next time.

- To help you remember which breast to begin with next feeding time, put a safety pin on that side of your bra or move a ring to that hand.

- You can feed your baby from both breasts each time, or you can feed your baby from one breast one time and the other breast the next time. Either way is perfectly fine. You will produce the most milk if your breasts are emptied during a feed.

- Feed your baby often at first to help your milk come in and prevent becoming engorged (see page 108).

- Avoid using a bottle or soother if you are breastfeeding. The two different sucking techniques confuse a baby.

- Nursing a baby every few hours is tiring work. If you can, ask someone else to burp and change the baby in between nursing sessions.

Breastfeeding

Breast milk, including the colostrum of the first few days, is perfectly suited to meet the needs of your baby. It has all the right ingredients, in just the right amounts, to help her growth. It is the perfect temperature, inexpensive and always available. In addition, breastfeeding helps you to lose weight, and stimulates your uterus to shrink back to normal size. Breastfeeding helps you to feel close to your baby.

At first, your breasts produce colostrum. This is a yellowish sticky milk-like substance. It is rich with vitamins, protein, and antibodies to protect your baby from infections. Newborns have a store of fat and water that they use up in the first few days of life. This explains why newborns lose weight at first. Colostrum alone is enough food for your baby for the first few days. There is no need to give your baby water or formula. Abundant milk will come in within 2-3 days.

When to start

The best time to start breastfeeding is within an hour or so after the birth when your newborn is very alert and ready to suck. Your nurses will ask if you want to breast-feed your baby, and will help you get started. Not all babies learn immediately how to nurse, but it is still a good idea to use this time to get breastfeeding started. Make sure you let the hospital staff know that you want your baby to stay in your room with you (rooming in) so you can nurse your baby whenever he seems hungry. Feeding your baby frequently helps to increase your milk supply.

Nursing positions

You can nurse your baby in many comfortable positions. Here are a few ideas:

Lying down

Lie in bed on your side, with your head on a couple of pillows. Lay the baby down beside your lower breast. Put a rolled up blanket or towel behind the baby's back.

Cradle hold

Find a comfortable sitting position. Prop a pillow under the arm that holds your baby. Put the baby's head at your breast with the baby's feet lying across your abdomen.

Football hold

Find a comfortable sitting position. Tuck the baby's legs under your arm so the feet point toward your back. Use a pillow to support the baby's head at the level of your breast. (This position puts less pressure on your abdomen if you had a caesarean birth.)

How to get started

It usually takes a bit of time for both you and your baby to learn how to breastfeed. Babies naturally want to suck. When you brush your finger across the baby's cheek, he will naturally turn his head toward you and open his mouth. When you put your nipple in the baby's mouth, the baby will start to suck. This causes milk to flow. For the first 24 hours, your baby will probably nurse about every 2–3 hours for three to five minutes on each breast. Or your baby may only nurse from one breast and stop.

Follow these steps to help you get started:

Step 1. Get comfortable.

Have pillows handy to support your arm, hold the baby close in the crook of your arm and point his face toward your breast; put your baby's abdomen against yours.

Step 2. Tease the baby.

Lift your breast with your free hand and point the nipple at the baby's mouth. Brush your nipple against the baby's lip, wait for the baby's lips to curl back and for the mouth to open WIDE (like a yawn). Then POP! the baby on to your nipple by quickly pushing the baby's head on to your breast. This movement is called getting your baby to latch on. Make sure that as much as possible of the areola, the dark pigmented skin around your nipple, is in the baby's mouth. The baby's nose and chin should be touching your breast. None of the areola, or only a small portion of it, should be visible around the baby's mouth. Babies who don't have enough of the areola in their mouths will suck only on your nipple. This may make your nipples very sore and the baby won't get enough milk. Latching on properly is one of the most important things you can do to make breastfeeding a success. If the baby does not latch on properly, break the suction and get the baby to latch on again.

Step 3. Breaking the suction.

To take the baby off your breast, slide your smallest finger inside the corner of the baby's mouth and push down a bit. This will break the suction seal. Do this every time you want to take the baby off your breast to prevent your nipples from becoming sore, then go back to Step 2 and try to get the baby to latch on again.

Common breastfeeding problems

Tender, sore breasts

Wear a properly fitting, full-support nursing bra all the time, even at night. Change nursing positions to put pressure on different parts of your nipples. Make sure both breasts get an even amount of nursing time. The best way to care for your breasts is to make sure your baby latches on properly, every time.

Sore nipples

During the first few days of nursing, it is normal for your nipples to feel tender when your baby first latches on to the breast. The tenderness, which lasts about 60 seconds after latching, usually disappears in the first week. If nipple pain increases or continues throughout the entire feeding or after the feeding, this is a warning that something is wrong.

Check with the nurses on the unit or your public health nurse to be sure your technique is good. Make sure the baby latches on properly. If she has not, break the seal and get the baby to latch on again. Begin nursing on the breast that feels the least sore. Nurse often, offering the breast as soon as the baby first seems interested. Crying is often a hunger cue—but by then she may be too frantically hungry to get a good latch.

To help heal the nipple, use an ointment provided when you were in hospital, or modified lanolin cream such as Pure-Lan or Lansinoh. Avoid the use of soaps, which dry out the skin and wash away the skin's natural oils. Spread breast milk over the nipples and let them dry in the air after each feed. Breast milk contains fat with antibacterial and antiviral properties and other substances that help heal and protect. Use cloth or paper breast pads in your bra to help absorb the leaking milk, but change them often so that they don't keep your nipples damp. Use a cold, wet towel or ice on your nipples between feeds to reduce swelling.

Engorgement

Breastfeeding is a matter of supply and demand. Breasts become engorged (very full of milk) when the supply is greater than the demands of the baby. After a while, your breasts learn how much milk is needed to satisfy your baby and will not produce extra. For this reason, it is important to feed your baby regularly and not to miss any feedings. Engorged breasts may be hard, lumpy, and painful because the swollen milk glands are very full of milk. They can be so swollen that the nipple becomes flat and hard for the baby to latch on to. In this case, you will need to express some milk to take the pressure off the breast and allow the flattened nipple room to stand up.

Blocked milk ducts

You may have a blocked milk duct if you notice one area of a breast that seems particularly tender, warm, and swollen. In this case, it is best to try to open the milk gland before nursing your baby, by putting warm wet towels on your breasts. Then massage your breasts in an effort to move the milk toward your nipples as you nurse your baby. Start under your arms. Make sure the baby latches on properly. Nurse your baby as often as possible to help keep the milk flowing. Increase the amount of fluids you are drinking to help flush out the milk ducts.

Take Tylenol® about 20 minutes before you begin nursing. After the feeding, put cold wet towels on your breasts to reduce swelling.

Mastitis

Mastitis is an infection of one or more milk glands in the breast. You may experience flu-like symptoms, fever and chills, and notice a reddened, hot spot on one or both breasts. Call your doctor right away. Mastitis is a serious infection that can be easily treated with antibiotics. Get plenty of rest.

Formula-feeding your baby

Breast milk is the best source of food for the first six months of your baby's life but giving your baby a commercially prepared, brand name formula is also a good way to feed your baby. Mothers who choose to formula-feed their babies also bond deeply with their babies.

Choosing the right formula

It is important to choose a commercially prepared brand name formula. If you are not sure which brand to use, ask your doctor or public health nurse. Most of these formulas are made from cows' milk that has been changed to be as close to breast milk as possible. Some babies have trouble digesting cow's-milk-based formulas. For these babies, soy-based formulas are a good substitute. Choose a formula that is recommended for newborns, and not a formula for older babies. Formula comes in three forms: as a powder you mix with water, as a concentrated liquid you mix equally with

water, and in a ready-to-serve form. Each of these forms gives your baby the same nourishment, if you mix them according to the instructions.

Sterilizing equipment

It is not always necessary to sterilize the equipment you will use to bottle-feed your baby, but it is very important to keep the equipment clean. Wash it well in hot, soapy water and rinse all the soap off. Leave it to air dry. Some mothers prefer to sterilize equipment until their babies are a few months old, or when their babies are sick. It is easy to sterilize the equipment. All you have to do is submerge all the equipment in a deep pot of water. Bring the water to a boil for five minutes. Remove the cooled equipment from the water with sterilized tongs (lifters) and fill them with formula.

Why babies cry

Newborns cry a lot until they are about two months old. Crying is the only real way that very young babies have to communicate their needs and feelings (hungry, wet, tired, lonely, uncomfortable, too warm, too cold, or frustrated in any other way).

Sometimes newborn crying seems entirely unrelated to basic need. Four out of five babies have daily crying sessions lasting from 15 minutes to an hour that are not easily explained. It can be very upsetting when you can't seem to find out what your baby needs. Sometimes, you will offer a feeding, a dry diaper, a cuddle, and everything else you can possibly think of, and she will still not stop crying. You may feel useless, frustrated, and even angry.

Some helpful tips to care for a crying baby:

Watch for signs of hunger (making sucking noises, turning head toward breast with open mouth) and feed a hungry baby before she starts to cry.

Pick up, rock, cuddle, hold, burp, and walk a fussy baby.

Massage her body, sing, coo, and talk to a lonely baby.

Check for a dirty diaper and change an uncomfortable baby.

Take layers of clothing off a warm baby (you can tell by feeling the temperature of the skin on a baby's tummy) and add layers of clothing to a cool baby.

Wrap a receiving blanket snugly around the over-tired baby to help her sleep.

Never shake your baby

Walk away

Call for help

109

Getting help when you cannot cope

It can be a very hard job to look after a baby. You may need help. It is okay to need help. Many new mothers do. To protect your baby, you must take control of the situation and get the help you need. Never shake your baby. Even treating your baby roughly, for example by throwing the baby into her crib, can cause brain damage.

If you are very angry and very frustrated... and you cannot cope for another second with your crying and fussing baby, you are at your wits' end and worried you may be losing your mind or losing control, or think you may hurt your baby...

Put your baby in a safe place! (in the crib or on the floor if the baby cannot crawl) and leave the room, close the door, walk to another part of the house, away from the crying baby (the baby will be fine for a few minutes even if she is crying).

Get control over your feelings... express your feelings by letting the rage out—hit a pillow, a mattress, yell, scream, and stomp your feet. Be angry without hurting the baby! Take a deep breath, relax, count slowly to 10. Get control of yourself!

Get help. Now. Call someone. Don't wait another minute! Call someone you trust or anyone who may be able to help you find the help you need:

- a friend, family member, or your partner
- the hospital where you had your baby
- the public health nurse or your doctor

Parenting classes

Classes to promote good parenting are available in most communities. These classes are recommended for everyone because they help to boost the confidence of new parents. Most importantly, they offer new parents a chance to share their experiences with other parents facing many of the same problems and joys. They are particularly helpful for first-time parents or very young new parents.

In these classes, you will learn basic parenting skills, such as feeding, diapering, and bathing, in addition to a variety of other topics such as child safety, sibling rivalry, and coping with frustration. If you and your partner recently arrived from another country, parenting classes may be useful in helping you to bridge the cultural differences you may face raising a child in Canada.

Most importantly, parenting classes may be very beneficial for you if, when you think back to your own childhood, you feel saddened by the way your parents raised you and you want to do a better job with your children. Now may be your chance to break the cycle and begin afresh with your own family, as you set out on the sometimes hard, always rewarding, job of raising a healthy, happy child.

Some Useful Internet Addresses

Canadian Paediatric Society	www.cps.ca
Canadian Institute of Child Health	www.cich.ca
Motherisk	www.motherisk.org
Lamaze International	www.lamaze-childbirth.com
La Leche League International	www.lalecheleague.org
HIV/AIDS in Pregnancy	www.cdnaids.ca www.thebody.com/whatis/women.shtml
Morning Sickness	http://health.ucsd.edu/guide/T0167.htm and www.motherisk.org
Women's Health (general)	www.stjosephs.london.on.ca/ SJHC/programs/women/women.htm
Twins/Multiple Birth	www.nomoct.org www.twinsmagazine.com
Nutrition for Healthy Term Infants (Health Canada Web Site)	www.hc-sc.gc.ca/hppb/childhood-youth/cfyh/nutrition and www.hc-sc.gc.ca/hppb/childhood-youth/cfyh/infantnutrition.htm

freedom of choice, 59
fumes, working with, 7

G

genetic testing, 22-23
genital herpes/warts, 13
German measles, 11, 19
gestational hypertension, 41, 52,
  see also high blood pressure
gravity, centre of, 33, 46
groin, pain in, 47
Group B streptococcus (GBS), 57

H

hair, of babies, 102
headaches, 26, 52
heads, of babies, 102
health care providers, 24
heart, see also under fetus
  exercise and, 31, 32
heartburn, 47
hemoglobin, 7, 19
hemorrhage
  during labour, 41
  postpartum, 86, 88
hemorrhoids, 46, 96
Hepatitis B, 19, 20
hereditary diseases, 11
high blood pressure, 73, see also
  gestational hypertension
  premature labour and, 39
HIV, see human immune deficiency
  virus
home care, 89
hormones, 2
  babies' sex organs and, 102
  depression and, 93
  ovulation and, 4
  placenta and, 3
  pregnancy, 16
  during second trimester, 36
  sex and, 31
  skin pigmentation and, 37
hospital
  length of stay in, 89
  preparing for, 66, 68

what to expect, 58-59
when to go, 74
hot tubs, 33
human chorionic gonadotrophin
  (HCG), 3
human immune deficiency virus
  (HIV), 13, 19, 21
hydrotherapy, 80
hypertension, 52, see also gestational
  hypertension

I

immature body systems, 42
implantation, 2
indigestion, 47
insulin, 29, 45, see also diabetes
intrauterine devices (IUDs), 14, 98
intravenous line (IV), 61
iron
  pregnancy and, 7, 8
  supplements, 46

J

jaundice, 104

K

Kegel exercises, 26, 34, 92, 96
kneeling, during delivery, 80

L

La Leche League, 53
labour, see also delivery
  body positions during, 79-80
  eating and drinking during, 62
  false, 43, 70, 76
  first stage, 76-82
  fourth stage, 87-88
  induced, 62, 69, 72-73
  movement during, 62
  pain control during, 5
  premature, 39-41, 43-44
  real vs. false, 70, 76
  second stage, 82-85
  signs of, 72

slow progress in, 76
stages of, 75
support during, 74-75
third stage, 86
labour coaches, 59, 61, 74, 79
  during active labour, 77
  during early labour, 76
  during third stage of labour, 86
  during transition to active labour, 78
labour support persons, 59, see also
  midwives; obstetrical nurses
lanolin cream, 108
latching on, 106, 107, 108
LDRP (labour, delivery, recovery, and
  postpartum) units, 58
lifestyle, of mothers, 5, 13, 21
lightening, 66
linea nigra, 37
liver disease, 20
lochia, 94
lotions, 48
lovemaking, see sexual relations
lungs
  of baby, 42, 50, 66
  exercise and, 31

M

mastitis, 109
maternal serum screening, 22
meconium, 75, 103
medical history, 5, 11-12
  fetal abnormalities and, 22
medication
  birth control pills, 97
  during labour, 61
  for nausea and vomiting, 25
  for pain relief, 81-82
  pregnancy and, 10
  sleeping pills, 68
menstrual cycle, 2, 4, 17, 94
metabolism, 97
  during first trimester, 26
midwives, 24, 58, 75
milk ducts, blocked, 108
milk glands, 16
milk supply, 106
miscarriages, 14, 27, 36